ME, MYSELF & IMPOSTOR

How to boss your Impostor Syndrome through 'The F.R.A.U.D. Framework™'

VANETTA MORRISON

To request permissions, contact the author at: vanetta@blueprintway.com

Paperback: 978-1-73-969300-8
Ebook: 978-1-73-969301-5
First Edition: September 2022

Cover Design by Sabrina Brown; Editing by Letitia Jeffers;
Graphic Design by Dr. Gyles Morrison

Published by: Vanetta Morrison
www.memyselfandimpostor.com

Legal disclaimer

This publication is meant as a source of valuable information for the reader, however it is not meant as a substitute for direct expert assistance.

If such a level of assistance is required, the services of a competent professional should be sought.

The author assumes no responsibility for errors, inaccuracies, omissions, or any other inconsistencies herein and hereby disclaims any liability to any party for any loss, damage, or disruption caused by errors or omissions, whether such errors or omissions result from negligence, accident, or any other cause.

Content Warning

This book references experiences of discrimination, racism and sexual abuse, which may be upsetting to some readers.

This book is dedicated to my darling daughter Anaya.

May your thoughts never imprison you
and may you break any chains the world
unjustly puts on you.
I'll always be in your corner.

Welcome

Hey lovely,

Thank you for buying my book!

I'm Vanetta Morrison, Director of The Blueprint Way™ - an online counselling and coaching service dedicated to helping Black & Brown women grow their emotional wealth, so they can thrive from the inside out.

I wrote this book especially for you, Black Women, Brown Women, Women of Colour, if you often find yourself doubting your abilities, even in the face of objective achievements.

Impostor Syndrome is partly like an internalised glass ceiling - a mix of self-sabotaging thoughts and feelings holding us back before anyone else even has the chance to. Another side of Impostor Syndrome is very much created and reinforced by our discriminating environments and the barriers racism, sexism and misogyny put on our progress, so I will be addressing both sides.

The framework presented in this book is your guide to:

- More clarity - through a deeper understanding of the different faces and triggers of Impostor Syndrome

- More confidence - as you see yourself and the power of your story in a new light and

- More competence - as you access and action an easy to remember formula to boss your Impostor Syndrome, both quickly and effectively

Through my personal and professional client stories as well as evidence-based psychological tools, I want to help you to:

- Recognise and call out the oppressive power of your environment and

- Control your inner critic by bossing your Impostor type

I hope you find the book useful.

Here, and honoured to help,

Contents

CHAPTER 1

Why Impostor Syndrome?

"I still have a little [bit of] impostor syndrome, it never goes away, that you're actually listening to me. It doesn't go away, that feeling that you shouldn't take me that seriously. What do I know? I share that with you because we all have doubts in our abilities, about our power and what that power is."

MICHELLE OBAMA

"I go through acute imposter syndrome with every role. I think winning an Oscar may in fact have made it worse. Now I've achieved this, what am I going to do next? What do I strive for? Then I remember that I didn't get into acting for the accolades, I got into it for the joy of telling stories."

LUPITA NYONG'O

"The Impostor syndrome follows everyone. I don't care, I mean, I feel like it's sort of a false narrative if I said that you know every time I get an award I just walk off the stage and I feel like the boss, I feel like it's affirmation. But in reality, those three words keep playing over and over in my head which is 'And now what?!' You start the next job, you get on that set and for a minute you feel like you're just starting all over again. You're going to be found out; that you're not as good as people think you are, you have an added responsibility, an added visibility – it's fear.

It's something that's deeply human I think."

VIOLA DAVIS

"I'm very insecure about my voice. After being told for so many years that you're not as good as this person or that person, it beats away on your insecurities ... I always wanted to be a singer and a dancer but when they start dissecting you like that, it does work away at your insecurities. You know? I'm like, 'Wow, I thought I was good at this.' It does get to you. I'm only human."

JENNIFER LOPEZ

None of the women above need much, if any, introduction. They are all household names and yet they all struggle with Impostor Syndrome - an experience 70% of humanity has shared or will share with them, me included.

My first encounter with Impostor Syndrome was in the autumn of 2016. I remember how it felt - my first project board meeting as a newly, double promoted, project manager. I had tried to dress the part - my hair in long, colour 1B,[1]crochet faux locs, wearing my trusted combination of some tailored blazer, a pretty blouse, black skinny jeans, and dress shoes. Something I hoped would express Girl Boss energy that (introvertedly) screamed both confidence and curiosity, resilience and reliability, style and sensibility.

On the inside, however, I felt stressed. I thought I might pass out, or puke, or both. My throat felt like it was closing in on me, so I kept reaching for my water bottle to keep my vocal cords ready, whenever the time came for me to speak.

As an Introvert, I was used to feeling those nervous butterflies in my stomach everytime before I said something. However, on the spectrum between Introvert[2] and Extravert[3], I am more in the middle, one could say I am an introverted Ambivert[4].

So, for the most part, I had learned to push past those butterflies, put on a brave smile, and dive into the conversation, before my brain could remind me of how daunting the situation really was.

But this time was different. After all, I was sitting around a table of senior stakeholders, one of which was a University Executive Board member[5] (think C-Suite for my US readers), who was the Project's Senior Responsible Owner.[6]

“

My first encounter with Impostor Syndrome was in the autumn of 2016. I remember how it felt - my first project board meeting as a newly, double promoted, project manager. I had tried to dress the part - my hair in long, colour 1B , crochet faux locs, wearing my trusted combination of some tailored blazer, a pretty blouse, black skinny jeans, and dress shoes.

”

They were looking at me to assert myself in my role. My role - Project Manager of a project that was missing its deadlines before I was even recruited. Project Manager of a project that was high stakes and core to the University's Admission and Enrolment figures and therefore core to its finances. Project Manager who felt like an Impostor. But, I'm getting ahead of myself - let's take it back six years.

It was the summer of 2010 when I graduated from my BA in Health Studies and Psychology with a 1st Class Honours degree. The world was my oyster and I had big dreams of completing a Phd, travelling the world and some day working for the UN.

But in reality, 16 years of non-stop studying, across 2 continents, 3 countries, 5 cities and 6 educational institutions from primary school all the way to university had left me physically and mentally exhausted. I just wanted (and definitely needed) a break. Lovely, rest is so important!

And because I decided to take the break in my university city, away from my family home, it also meant getting a job to fund my so-called study break. I now laugh at the thought that taking a break from studies for me at the time meant finding a full-time job, but that's how it felt then.

I managed to get a temp job straight out of uni, and unknowingly started the slow climb up the corporate ladder. After a year, I switched from a temp assistant contract to a permanent administrator one, but other than that, nothing changed in my career for the next 5 years.

It wasn't for my lack of trying though. Aware of the fact that I was soon working below my abilities, and outside of my field of interest (in my final year of studies, I had decided I wanted to be a counsellor), I applied to many more suitable roles, unsuccessfully. The one thing I never considered was becoming a manager where I was, because I didn't want to be where I was for much longer.

However, this is where opportunities started developing for me. From time to time positions would come up that required more of my abilities (something the high achiever in me loved) and that paid more (something my bank account loved).

Yet, true to the desire of many of my millennial peers, I wanted my next job to be more meaningful to me, to bring me closer to my passion, to help me fulfil my purpose.

I didn't like the idea of doing something I didn't really want to do, just for the sake of a management title and more money. I wanted a job that both paid my bills and set my soul on fire. Was that really asking for too much?!

At the time, my reluctance to apply had nothing to do with my confidence level and everything to do with my passion level. I knew I could manage projects and a team, especially as I was already doing it voluntarily at my local church.

Yet, the doors I wanted to have opened, kept being and staying shut. The one door I wasn't interested in was like a revolving one, bringing me back to the opportunity to manage where I was already working.

By the summer of 2016, I had made a few observations that ultimately changed my mind about applying for a management job in my department.

Observation 1: For many professions, having a Bachelor's Degree isn't enough to set you up to become a professional in your field of choice.

I had held on to the belief that all I needed was a BA to start my graduate entry into my dream career. But with so many of my millennial peers also having Bachelor degrees, employers were expecting more of their applicants than good degrees and some relevant voluntary work.

I needed experience in the field, but I wasn't experienced enough to gain the experience, so for a while I found myself growing despondent and more emotionally exhausted.

Observation 2: Your network determines your access.

The reason why opportunities were coming my way where I was, was because people knew, liked and trusted me and more importantly, my work.

After uni, I inadvertently took a break from the world of psychology and counselling and focused on University Admissions instead. As I didn't cultivate the contacts I had had while studying, by the time I was ready to re-enter that world, no one really knew me. I had to start from scratch, building and cultivating my network in that field. But where I already was, that network was thriving.

Observation 3: It's okay to follow the favour

Having spent 6 years knocking on doors that refused to open, I started feeling like I was being unwise, hoping for change, but not acting on the one opportunity that kept presenting itself to me, like it was destined for me.

Turns out, it was.

It just so happened that I was given the opportunity to deputise for my manager for a day and it all went so well that day that I decided to at least consider any future management position in my department. But only if it was offered to me by my manager and by my manager's manager.

A month after my silent resolve to God, our department received an internal email from my manager's manager advertising an acting-up project management role. Not long after the email, my manager took me to the side to personally ask me whether I'd apply for the role, as she genuinely believed I should.

As far as I was concerned, my conditions of consideration had been met, so, finally following the one persistent area of favour in my work life, I applied to a management role 2 levels above my current one at the time, with no doubt in my mind that I could do the job.

That is, until I got and started the job.

Suddenly, the Vanetta who had been fairly confident in her academic and professional abilities her whole life up to this point, started becoming an anxious and burned-out shell of herself, wondering how long it would take her new manager to recognise she had made a mistake in promoting her, because Vanetta was actually an incapable fraud who must have somehow just charmed her way into this position, as well as any previous voluntary management positions.

The fact that a month into my role I had already successfully project managed the office move of 3 teams and was a pivotal point of contact for the move of the rest of the department, somehow seemed irrelevant during my meltdown. All I could sense was the demise of the image of the Strong Black Woman I had of myself and unbeknownst to me then, the ascent of my Impostor Syndrome.

My second encounter with Impostor Syndrome came 3 years after the first one, at which point, I had swapped my employed manager title to that of self-employed entrepreneur. I had eventually found my stride as a manager 6-8 months into my new role, feeling confident, competent and connected to my team. And I was clearly doing well enough as I was soon asked to train my deputy to replace me, so I could manage another, bigger, more critical team to cover business needs.

Although this transition was much smoother than the previous, by the time I left the role a year and a half later, I had once again become an anxious, crying shell of myself. This time it was triggered by a poorly managed and personally embarrassing and traumatising restructure[7] process.

I was busy trying to both protect my team from the mental distress of the restructure as well as keep them productive while dealing with new, inadequate IT systems. And although I will never regret putting my team first, at the time I failed to successfully re-interview for a management job I had already been doing, and doing well, for 3 years.

So, unless I could find a new job asap, because my management jobs were only ever acting up positions, I was faced with a double demotion back down to my permanent Administrator role, including a £10,000 ($13,400 or €12,000) pay cut. Of course, I did apply for other jobs, but the very few I got invited to interview for, I didn't get.

As the deadline for me to be demoted kept drawing closer, without what seemed like a way out, I increasingly felt devastated, distressed, embarrassed, heart-broken and ashamed. But that is not what made me feel like an Impostor - that came soon after.

The morning of September 23rd, 2019, my 32nd birthday, my husband, Gyles, received a phone call that changed the trajectory of both of our lives.

The call was to confirm that he had been successful in securing what seemed like an incredible job opportunity which would require us relocating to Germany - my country of birth and upbringing.

Due to a convergence of circumstances which included the demotion deadline creeping up, our sudden and exciting emigration plans, as well as me successfully completing my counselling practitioner accreditation, I unexpectedly found myself back in Germany, setting up my own counselling and coaching practice.

As I anxiously wrestled with this new title of entrepreneur while processing the trauma of my last experience of being an employee, I came across the concept of Impostor Syndrome, and immediately everything fell into place.

I finally understood why I had been feeling how I was when I first started as a manager and how I was feeling now as an entrepreneur. I finally had appropriate language for what was going on with how I saw myself.

As I continued to do my research into Impostor Syndrome, my psychology training and management experience kicked in.

I developed a framework to help myself and the many people I knew personally and professionally, who knowingly and unknowingly struggle with Impostor Syndrome, boss it, instead of letting it boss them.

This is how The F.R.A.U.D. Framework™ was born.

Since its inception in spring 2020, I have helped hundreds of people - entrepreneurs, PhD students, clinicians, designers, mompreneurs, artists, managers etc. learn to boss their Impostor Syndrome, both through 1:1 sessions, group workshops and a short eBook.

Here are some of their stories:

"I booked Vanetta's impostor syndrome coaching [workshop] for a group of female theology researchers. From my point of view as an Equal Opportunities Officer at a university, the coaching [and training] by Vanetta is a deep dive that provides a completely new insight on career issues: [the workshop] uncovered obstacles that not only (but also) affect structural aspects. [...] Vanetta's work is characterized by its high level of professionalism. I strongly recommend collaboration with her."

ALEKSANDRA BRAND

Equal Opportunities Officer, PhD Candidate & Lecturer at University of Bochum

The Impostor Syndrome workshop was an enlightening and enjoyable session helping to identify your own frailties and how to best deal with the different presentations of Impostor Syndrome.

Fantastic facilitation throughout the session and it felt like a safe space to share thoughts, ideas, and experiences. Would definitely recommend it.

DR OLIVER ADEBAYO

Orthopaedic Registrar

The Workshop on Impostor Syndrome with Vanetta Morrison made me finally understand why I've felt this strange feeling for most of my adult and professional life and provided me with an easy and structured framework to deal with this.
I highly recommend this simple approach!

DR ANDREI VASILE
Obstetrics and Gynaecology Resident

"The 1st, 2nd and 3rd step [of the framework] were the most useful to me as they outlined some of the lies I was telling myself which made me doubt and compare myself to others. These parts helped me to reshape my thinking and to see the written truths that I'm a quite accomplished person and I'm more than capable to achieve my goals."

TRACY AMOFA-DIATUO
Dietician Nutritionist

"I couldn't recommend this enough, especially as someone who likes short, sharp, straight to the point solutions, it ticks all of those boxes. Thank you for making your tools easily accessible to the world. I can't think of a single person who wouldn't benefit from this!"

AMINATA KAMARA
BBC Radio Presenter & Producer

Thank you Vanetta for such an insightful course. It was packed with great information and tools that could be taken away and applied. Impostor syndrome uncovered and confronted within a small group of like-minded women. No doubts for me, I would highly recommend this course to anyone struggling with Impostor Syndrome.

ANONYMOUS

This weekend workshop was excellent. The amount of people in the session allowed for it to remain intimate and for bonds to be quickly formed. I felt that I left the weekend with practical tools that I could use to fight Impostor Syndrome and the booklet means I always have something to look back on.

ANONYMOUS

Through this book, I'm passionate about helping millions more free themselves from the negative consequences of Impostor Syndrome and instead leverage and build on the positive aspects.

I look forward to hearing your stories of bossing your Impostor Syndrome.

Endnotes

1 Colour 1B: A popular colour name for hair extensions which matches many Black women's natural Black hair colour (*For a complete glossary, see page 213)*

2 Introvert: someone who draws energy most from quiet or solitary activities

3 Extravert: someone who draws energy most from social activities

4 Ambivert: someone who can equally draw energy from both solitary and/or social activities

5 Executive Board Member: a key decision maker in a business, member of the board of directors

6 Senior Responsible Owner: owner of the project's business case; primarily owns any risks of the project and responsible for ensuring the project meets its objectives

7 Restructure: a process taken by a business that involves the significant modification of a department's previous ways of operating in order to make it more efficient

CHAPTER 2

What in the world is Impostor Syndrome?

What we call Impostor Syndrome today was initially referred to as *Impostor Phenomenon* when it was first defined in the 1970s. Over time, other names have been used to label the phenomenon, including *perceived fraudulence, impostorism* and *fraud syndrome*.

Psychotherapists Dr. Pauline Clance and Dr. Suzanne Imes published their initial piece of research on Impostor Phenomenon in 1978 based on their observations of high achieving women, some of which were their therapy clients. They defined Impostor Phenomenon as the "...internal experience of intellectual phoniness."[1]

Based on my research and review of literature, I define Impostor Syndrome as:

"a persistent experience of ***inadequacy, incompetence*** *and* ***context-specific isolation*** *in which objective successes are discounted or attributed to anything other than personal effort and ability."*

I know, it's a mouthful. But, we'll walk through the definition's different keywords (in bold) throughout the book. It will make sense in the end, I promise.

In 1985, Dr. Pauline Clance identified six potential symptoms of Impostor Phenomenon and stated that to be considered an Impostor, at least two of the below symptoms should be present:

1. the Impostor Cycle
2. the need to be special or to be the very best
3. Superman/Superwoman aspects
4. fear of failure
5. denial of competence and discounting praise and
6. fear and guilt of success.[2]

Let's have a closer look at some of these symptoms now. The rest will be referred to later in the book.

“

Impostor Syndrome is a persistent experience of inadequacy, incompetence and context-specific isolation in which objective successes are discounted or attributed to anything other than personal effort and ability.

”

1. The Impostor Cycle

According to Dr. Clance the Impostor Cycle (see Figure 1 below) is one of the top symptoms of Impostor Phenomenon.

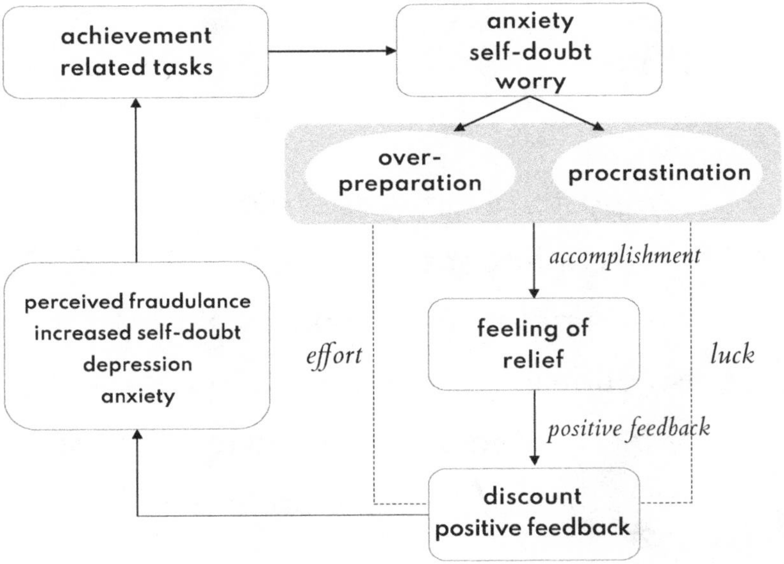

Figure 1: The Imposter Cycle, based on Clance (1985a)

The cycle begins with the assigning of an achievement related task, for example an academic essay or a work project. This triggers anxiety and self doubt in the individual with Impostor fears.

The anxious person then tries to cope with the anxiety through either extreme overpreparation, or initial procrastination, followed by panicked preparation.

Next, they successfully complete the task and for a time feel relief and a sense of accomplishment. However, those positive feelings soon make way for negative ones, as the person discounts their personal contribution to the successful task completion, even in the face of positive feedback from others.

According to the view of the Impostor, if they over-prepared, their achievement was down to hard work, which they don't believe is a true sign of ability. And if they procrastinated, then their achievement was only down to luck.

Either way, they feel like they are a fraud which increases their self doubt and can also lead to depression and anxiety. This is then the context in which a new task is assigned, starting the cycle of reinforcing their impostor feelings and anxiety all over again.

2. Fear of failure

Fear of failure has been identified as a subconscious experience of most Impostors[3]. This is why overworking is a strategy many Impostors adopt, to reduce the risk of failure and to avoid experiencing correlating feelings of shame and humiliation.

3. Denial of competence and discounting praise

Impostors are not trying to fish for compliments or humble brag when they discount praise or deny their competence. Instead, it has been shown in many studies, that people living with Impostor fears ascribe their success to external factors more, than people who don't live with Impostor fears[4].

They genuinely don't believe they deserve any praise and in fact even try to find evidence that they don't.

This is because they don't believe overworking or procrastination are acceptable paths towards achievement. Even when the end result is success, for many Impostors, instead of the end (success) justifying the means (overwork or procrastination), the means invalidate the end or at least their personal contribution to it.

This is why, despite me having a lot of self doubt during my university studies, I can see I didn't really veer into Impostor territory then. I used to procrastinate doing my university assignments all the time, but I never discounted my contribution to success when I ended up with a good grade.

In fact, I eventually just accepted procrastination as an integral part of my essay writing success mechanism at the time, because the one time I didn't procrastinate, was the one time I got a much lower grade. This is not an endorsement for procrastination by the way - there have been many occasions since, where it has been more of a curse than a blessing. I'll address this more at a later point in the book.

4. Fear and guilt about success

Impostors experiencing fear or guilt about success are acutely aware of the possible negative consequences of their success. One of these consequences can be a threat to their sense of belonging and community, which are both intrinsically tied to a person's sense of identity and safety.

If we can't identify as belonging to a community, we feel alone, exposed and even as though we have no purpose. Most people don't want to be or feel lonely and research has shown that loneliness negatively affects our mental health. Bottom line, belonging to a community is better for our mental health.

For Impostors if their successes are seen as 'abnormal' in the context of their family or friendship circles, it can leave them feeling anxious about being rejected and being isolated due to their difference.

By 'abnormal' I mean whatever breaks the mould of what has been deemed the norm or culture in their circles. This would include if they are the first or the only in their tribes to: go to university; pursue a career in Arts or Performing Arts (shout out to all my readers who had to convince their parents those are acceptable options); become an entrepreneur; become a white collar worker; become a blue collar worker etc.

Especially for people who already feel marginalised most of the time, it's near impossible to potentially jeopardise the only place they feel like they belong in pursuit of success without feeling afraid or guilty.

Another negative consequence is fearing that with continual success, higher demands will be made and greater expectations placed on the Impostor and they will eventually be revealed as the fraud they already think they are.

These 6 key symptoms are what differentiate Impostor Syndrome from the everyday self-doubt most of us experience at one point or another in our lives, especially in new or challenging situations.

Based on all 6 key indicators, Clance developed the *Clance Impostor Phenomenon Scale* - a self-assessment tool to help you identify whether you have any of the IP characteristics and if yes, how severe they are[5].

Total scoring is out of 100 and the higher the score, the more frequent someone experiences Impostor feelings and the more Impostor Phenomenon obstructs someone's life.

Scoring 60 or above is considered as worth a true 'diagnosis' of Impostor Syndrome. A free online version of the tool can be found here[6].

The first time I did the test, just before one of my workshops, my score was 54 - just below the threshold. But it goes to show that even though I train people on Impostor Syndrome, I have to continually do the work to ensure it doesn't hold me back. And I bet if I had known about the test back in 2016 or even 2020, before The F.R.A.U.D Framework™, those scores would have been much higher.

Since the initial research in 1978, more recent research has found that at least 70% of people will experience or already have experienced one episode of Impostor Syndrome in their lives[7]. With Impostor Syndrome having such a wide-spread impact on humanity, it is important to understand Impostor Syndrome better and identify how it got here in the first place.

Endnotes

1 Clance & Imes (1978)

2 Clance (1985a)

3 Clance & O'Toole (1988)

4 Sakulku & Alexander (2011)

5 Clance (1985b)

6 http://impostortest.nickol.as/

7 Sakulku & Alexander (2011)

CHAPTER 3

How did we get here?

Initial research proposed that the origins of Impostor Syndrome (IS) lie in *"certain early family dynamics and later introjection of societal sex-role stereotyping"* (Clance & Imes, 1978).

In other words, Clance & Imes initially believed IS occured when we are conditioned from birth to accept unrealistic, gender-specific expectations regarding achievement, success, and failure from our immediate family, who themselves learn these same expectations from their families, reinforced by society. As we get older and directly interact with society ourselves, these expectations also become reinforced in us.

This "societal sex role stereotyping" is why it was initially believed women experienced IS more, as society at the time did not consider intellectual or professional success as inherently womanly or feminine, affecting socialisation[1].

Our socialisation influences who we think we are and what we deserve. Aside from sex or gender roles, this can also be based on what

“

Our socialisation influences who we think we are and what we deserve. Aside from sex or gender roles, this can also be based on what social class, race, physical or mental health status etc. we relate to. Anytime we want to break out of these set characters assigned to us, we might feel a massive bout of Impostor Syndrome.

”

social class, race, physical or mental health status etc. we relate to. Anytime we want to break out of these set characters assigned to us, we might feel a massive bout of Impostor Syndrome.

So for example, if your family has consistently been typecast as lower class or lower middle class, but you have aspirations to level up in your social class, on your journey towards attaining middle to upper class and the change in lifestyle those classes represent, you may end up feeling like an Impostor.

Impostor Syndrome then becomes a symptom of challenging your socialisation by seeking to move away from your defined social role and the expectations of that role.

To note, the unrealistic expectations set by family and/or society could be both unrealistically high, expecting us to be able to excel in everything; or unrealistically low, not expecting much from us at all.

In either case, we may end up thinking we are an Impostor because we can't achieve as easily as our environment expects us to; or because we are achieving beyond our environment's expectations of us. In the latter case, we question if things have been made easy for us to succeed, or if we have just charmed our way into succeeding[2].

In addition to one's upbringing being considered a potential Impostor Syndrome trigger, research has also shown that some people possess personality traits that correlate strongly with Impostor Syndrome, such as:

- neuroticism
- perfectionism
- generalised anxiety
- high level of ambition[3].

So, not only can Impostor Syndrome occur due to your nurture/socialisation, you could also be more prone to experience Impostor Syndrome due to your nature/personality. This is why a multi-faceted solution is needed to help you boss it.

Impostor Syndrome and Mental Illnesses

Impostor Syndrome is not a classified mental illness[4], but in the initial research on Impostor Phenomenon (IP), Clance & Imes found that people with high IP also experience "generalised anxiety, lack of self-confidence and depression" [5], findings which have been replicated since[6].

So, although Impostor Syndrome (IS) itself is not a classified mental illness, it seems to significantly correlate with some classified mental illnesses, such as depression and anxiety.

This insight is especially important when considering successful treatment of IS, a reason why researchers are beginning to advocate for IS to be included in the next edition of the Diagnostic and Statistical Manual of Mental Disorders (DSM)[7] - the bible of standard assessment criteria and diagnosis of psychological and psychiatric disorders. A mental illness is not classified as one, unless it is in the DSM.

Impostor Syndrome and Gender Differences

Clance & Imes initial research proposed that Impostor Phenomenon was primarily an issue for high achieving, middle- to upper-class, predominantly White Women, and stated that men experienced it less frequently and/or less intensely.

With the introduction of the *Clance Impostor Phenomenon Scale*, intensity of one's Impostor experience could be quantified, with higher scores meaning higher intensity[8].

Much research since then has proven Impostor Syndrome is a cross-cultural, cross-generational, cross-class and cross-gender issue[9;10;11]).

That being said, despite great advances in women's rights over the last 50+ years, society by and large still considers women to be primary caregivers[12;13]. This has proven itself again during the COVID-19 pandemic starting in early 2020.

Before the pandemic, women were already doing 3 times more unpaid care and domestic work than men - this unpaid workload has just increased with school closures and self-isolation requiring home-schooling and home care[14].

The negative economic impact the Covid-19 pandemic has had particularly for women shows that although many women are flourishing in their careers, society generally still requires them to prioritise care duties in times of crisis.[15]

In other words, as women, we might be able to *have* it all, but only if we can *do* it all and *be* it all as well. With that sort of pressure, who wouldn't be feeling like an Impostor most of the time?! It's like constantly feeling ***inadequate*** is considered the fair price of admission by society for ambitious women.

“

It’s like constantly feeling inadequate is considered the fair price of admission by society for ambitious women.

”

Before I continue, I'm adding a content warning here. I'll be talking about the experiences women have with sexism and misogyny which can possibly be distressing to you. Should you feel distressed, please consider taking a break and engaging in self-soothing or mindfulness activities such as deep breathing exercises, progressive muscle relaxation, listening to calming music, speaking to a trusted friend, etc.

Let's not forget the experiences of sexism and misogyny women are exposed to persistently which are intended to make us feel inadequate and worthless.

Sexism is *"the belief that the members of one sex are less intelligent, able, skilful, etc. than the members of the other sex, especially that women are less able than men"*[16].

Misogyny on the other hand is defined as *"hatred, dislike, or mistrust of women, manifested in various forms such as physical intimidation and abuse, sexual harassment and rape, social shunning and ostracism,"*[17].

Both constructs negatively affect women's lives, but to varying degrees. The fact women are still predominantly paid less for the same type and duration of work than men is due to sexist ideologies and institutions.

But, what has caught media attention more in recent months and years are heart-breaking reports of women continually being abducted, raped, killed, tortured, physically and sexually abused etc.

Those are reports of misogynistic behaviours.

The sexist doesn't hate women, the misogynist does. The sexist is academic in their discrimination, the misogynist is visceral, but both sides contribute to the upkeep of a system oppressive towards women[18].

So, both individually and institutionally, viscerally and morally, we women are faced with the message that we don't belong or that we are frauds whenever we step outside the box of what is generally expected of us - which is being a nurturer.

This leads us back to the start of this section on why COVID-19 has reminded us that society is still by and large sexist, expecting women to be the most competent at caregiving and therefore mostly moving the burden of care on us.

Within a workplace context, results from a study commissioned by Access Commercial Finance in 2018 suggest that the gender distribution of Impostor Syndrome in the UK isn't actually equal. In their study, Access Commercial Finance found that 66% of women experienced Impostor Syndrome within the 12 month duration of the study, in contrast to 56% of men[19].

Now, a 10% difference may not seem that quantitatively significant, but it can make a huge difference qualitatively. An advisor connected to the study pointed out that the difference didn't just stop with employed women versus employed men.

When business lending data was considered, although more business loans were granted to women entrepreneurs in contrast to men entrepreneurs, women generally asked for business loans less, or asked for less money when they did ask, due to Impostor Syndrome[20].

As small as the gender difference with Impostor Syndrome may be in numbers, it may have huge negative repercussions on the career or business development of many women.

Impostor Syndrome and Race

I'm adding another content warning here as I will be discussing race-related and intersectional inequalities and oppression which might be distressing to some readers.

Initial research on the impact of race and ethnicity on Impostor Syndrome identified it is a cross-racial phenomenon, i.e. every people group experiences Impostor Syndrome (IS) similarly often[21].

However, once again, more recent research is showing that although there may be no racial differences in the fact that people *are* experiencing IS, race and ethnicity may contribute to a difference in *how* and at *what* level of severity IS is impacting people's lives[22;23].

One research study found IS was a greater indicator of psychological distress in Black students attending predominantly white universities, than minority status stress i.e., racism and discrimination[24].

This means the psychological wellbeing of those Black students was more negatively affected by Impostor Syndrome, than by their experiences with racism.

Another study identified that the interaction of IS and Minority Status Stress (MSS) creates a more distressing psychological burden for Black students and that experiencing MSS can often trigger feelings of Impostorism[25].

So, not only does IS mentally harm some students more than racism, for other students, racism itself can make some students feel like they are an Impostor.

Away from student populations, research has shown that in the workplace women of colour in particular experience Impostor Syndrome in more severe ways - this is likely due to the fact that:

1. women of colour live at the intersection of different forms of oppression and discrimination[26] and

2. IS can often be triggered when *"we don't see many examples of people who look like us [...] clearly succeeding in our field"*[27], an experience which women of colour know all too well.

A 2021 report by McKinsey & Company and LeanIn.org identified that in Corporate America Black Women are more than three times as likely and Latina and Asian Women more than twice as likely as White Women[28] to be exposed to microinsults concerning their language skills or other abilities[29].

In detail, the report showed that in a professional context, 18% of Black Women, 13% of Latinas and 11% of Asian Women are confronted by other people actually verbally expressing their 'positive surprise' at their eloquence, articulation and/or other skills. Talk about being patronising!

It makes me wonder how much higher the number is if it included people who also think that professional communication or other skills are not what they expect from Black & Brown women, but do not verbalise it to their Black & Brown Woman colleagues.

In relation to Impostor Syndrome, this report finding feeds into why Black Women may feel more ***incompetent*** than others, when on average almost every 5th woman is faced with openly expressed surprise when we do show competence.

Then we have the *'pet-to-threat'* narrative which many women of colour can face too. Coined by Professor Kecia Thomas in 2013, the 'pet-to-threat' phenomenon describes a particular experience Black women face that negatively impacts their career development[30].

This experience begins with the hiring of a woman of colour (WOC) at a junior level of her career at which point she is considered a beloved pet, rather than as a professional[31].

In a lecture for the Gender Summit presented on 14 November, 2013, Prof Thomas explained the process of the pet to threat transition[32]:

1. The WOC is likely hired because of her diversity and made a token within her context

2. Although leadership initially reacts positively towards her, showering her with recognition and rewards, the WOC herself starts to quickly feel overexposed, patronised and underutilised

3. As the WOC begins to establish herself in her career, challenges her pet status and grows in competence, experience and seniority, she is faced with the sudden transition from overprotected pet to perceived threat

4. Despite high levels of performance, the WOC faces barriers to progression as her leaders' previous overprotection has now been swapped for them questioning her achievements and success

5. The questioning and blocking of access to promotion can escalate to hostility and overt discrimination in the form of microaggressions towards the WOC

Ultimately, both the pet and the threat type casting negatively affects women of colour in their career progression as their social environment either ignores or discredits their abilities.

This forms a unique breeding ground for Impostor Syndrome, where actual ability and successes are questioned, but being a token of diversity receives performative praise.

That is because many company leadership teams want their staff to appear diverse, but not to actually do the work of increasing diversity, equity and inclusion.

Another potentially distressing topic Black women may deal with is the issue of misogynoir. Remember misogyny - the hatred of women often expressed viscerally?

Well misogynoir is the distrust, hatred of, and violence towards Black women as seen in pop culture and proliferated in the historical and current daily experiences of Black women[33].

The term was coined in 2008 by Moya Bailey, an Associate Professor of Communications, to describe the intersectional experience Black women have with anti-Black racism and misogyny, distinct from the misogynistic experiences women in general or women of colour more specifically have[34].

If just *being* a Black woman is already met with such opposition, how much more when we are *achieving* Black women?

Whether it is because of hostility, discrimination or exclusion, being consistently faced with decision making tables where no one looks like us or where our competence is questioned, can make us Black and Brown women question our sense of legitimacy and belonging, which is a core symptom of Impostor Syndrome.

“

Whether it is because of hostility, discrimination or exclusion, being consistently faced with decision making tables where no one looks like us or where our competence is questioned, can make us Black and Brown women question our sense of legitimacy and belonging, which is a core symptom of Impostor Syndrome.

”

A 2020 systematic review of published research on Impostor Syndrome (IS) has highlighted the need for a more 'culturally adjusted' clinical definition of IS based on evidence suggesting that for ethnic minorities there may be a *'racial component of impostor feelings'*[35].

Our experiences of being isolated within certain settings, be it because of our race, gender, disability, sexuality etc. or all of the above, feed into our experience of feeling like a fraud. This is why I talk about ***'context-specific isolation'*** in my definition of Impostor Syndrome.

This is also why representation is so important, because it helps us feel less isolated and more like we belong in the spaces we choose to occupy.

I talk about this point some more when discussing different ways our environment can trigger our Impostor Syndrome.

Finally, as a Black woman myself, this is why I focus primarily on supporting women of colour in bossing Impostor Syndrome.

Although everyone can and will benefit from applying the framework in this book, especially as Black & Brown women we spend most of our lives at an intersection of real, multifaceted oppression AND unrealistic societal expectations wrapped in racism, sexism and misogyny.

This can lead to an experience of persistent inadequacy, incompetence and isolation, aka Impostor Syndrome.

Key Ideas

- Impostor Syndrome (IS) = persistent experience of inadequacy, incompetence and isolation despite objective successes
- Both nature (personality) and nurture (socialisation) can increase prevalence of Impostor feelings
- IS: a cross-cultural, cross-generational, cross-class and cross-gender issue
- Pressure exists that women can *have* it all, only if they can *do* and *be* it all too
- High correlation of IS with depression & anxiety
- IS could be a stronger predictor of mental health issues than racism
- Women of colour living at the intersection of racism, sexism and misogyny are particularly prone to IS

Endnotes

1 Socialisation: a process of being taught the cultural and social norms of the community one grows up in

2 Clance & Imes (1978)

3 Sakulku & Alexander (2011)

4 Mental Illness: health condition involving changes in emotion, thinking or behaviour, associated with distress and/ or problems functioning in social, work or family activities.

5 Clance & Imes (1978)

6 Cusak et al. (2013)

7 Bravata et al. (2020)

8 Clance (1985b)

9 September et al. (2001)

10 Ghorbanshirodi (2012)

11 Peteet et al. (2015)

12 Swinkels et al. (2019)

13 Sharma et al. (2016)

14 UN Womens (2021)

15 Clance & Toole (1988)

16 Cambridge Dictionary (2021)

17 Dictionary.com (2021)

18 Prasad (2019)

19 FundingGuru.com (2018)

20 FundingGuru.com (2018)

21 Bravata et al. (2020)

22 Cokley et al. (2013)

23 McClain et al. (2016)

24 Cokley et al. (2013)

25 McClain et al. (2016)

26 Clance et al. (1995)

27 Nance-Nash (2020)

28 and also twice/three times as likely as men in general

29 McKinsey & Company (2021)

30 Donahue et al. (2021)

31 Stallings (2020)

32 Thomas (2013)

33 Trudy (2014)

34 Bailey & Trudy (2018)

35 Bravata et al. (2020)

CHAPTER 4

Impostor Subtypes

Content Warning

To boss Impostor Syndrome, it is important to understand the different ways it can show up practically in our day to day lives.

In this chapter we will start looking at the practical ways we may experience Impostor Syndrome ourselves which can possibly be distressing to you. Should you feel distressed, please consider taking a break and engaging in self-soothing or mindfulness activities such as deep breathing exercises, progressive muscle relaxation, listening to calming music, speaking to a trusted friend, etc.

Should you find it too hard to carry on reading, but are still interested in learning about the content, feel free to get in touch with me. We can arrange for 1:1 counselling sessions to help you process the distress and you can sign up to one of my small group workshops to learn techniques in a safe and confidential space.

Subtype Origins

An expert on the subject of Impostor Syndrome (IS), Dr. Valerie Young has conducted decades of research examining fraudulent feelings among high achievers.

From her research, Dr. Young identified different ways symptoms of IS show up and collated them into 5 Impostor subtypes:

- The Perfectionist
- The Expert
- The Natural Genius
- The Superhero/ Superwoman/ Superman/ Superstudent
- The Soloist[1]

We'll be looking at the different types in more detail now. If you'd like to identify your Impostor type, I created a quiz you can take here: **https://blueprintway.com/is-quiz/**

The Perfectionist

The Perfectionist Impostor Type thrives on seeking the perfect solution to any problems they face. They define success as nothing less than perfection and therefore feel like they have failed when achieving anything below that.

Referring back to Clance's 6 symptoms of Impostor Phenomenon, the Perfectionist resonates highly with the *'fear of failure'* symptom. This might be because as a child failure was never deemed acceptable and criticism was a constant.

If our caregivers did not provide us with a sense of physical and emotional security in our childhood through their consistent affection, care and validation, even in the face of us making mistakes, as adults we may now wrestle with those consequences, one of which may be perfectionism, or the anxiety to do things perfectly.

Now, as an adult, you feel like your work is never good enough and even when it is, you dismiss the work you put in and assume it is down to luck.

With all that pressure you put on yourself, sometimes you end up procrastinating on tasks, because you don't know how to start perfectly, so you'd rather not start at all.

If you are in a leadership position, you might also be accused of being a micromanager[2] – because you don't trust that a task will still be perfect if it isn't done by you and/or in your way. If you struggle with feeling the need to control everything and everyone around you, you might have this Impostor Type.

The Perfectionist Impostor Type differs from the person with perfectionism as a personality trait in that the latter tries hard to cover their imperfections, while the former openly confesses to them[3].

The Expert

The Expert thrives on having all the required knowledge to solve any problems they face. They define success as knowing everything therefore feel like they have failed when they lack knowledge in even the smallest things.

As an Expert, you don't feel satisfied with your academic achievements because there is always more to learn. You even downplay all you have already achieved. You feel very uncomfortable being referred to as an expert because no matter how much you know, you are acutely aware of how much more there is to know.

When looking for a job, you likely avoid applying for any role that you don't meet every requirement for, even the non-essentials. If you are in a leadership position, your feelings of Impostor Syndrome might be even more intense, because people are regularly seeking out your expertise. So, you often end up enrolling on all the degrees, courses, and training opportunities you can, so as not to be found out as the fraud you think you are.

The Natural Genius

The Natural Genius thrives on being able to solve any problems they face with ease and speed. They define success as being naturally able to learn and do something well on their 1st attempt. Therefore, they feel like they have failed when they are unable to master a subject or skill on their first try.

Going back to the 6 symptoms of Impostor Phenomenon Clance pointed out (Clance, 1985a), the Natural Genius connects well with the symptom of *'the need to be special, to be the very best'*.

This is because, as a child, you may have grown up being called special because with little effort on your part you did well in academics, athletics or arts, or a selection of them all. You were different to those around you and you likely never had to attribute your good achievements to hard work.

Now, whenever you are faced with something you can't do with ease, you may feel like you are a fraud and failure in that area.

This negative feeling is reinforced if you meet fellow Natural Geniuses who are succeeding in your area of struggle with ease and speed, and can lead to you discounting your success, because it is no longer special.

Whether in a personal or professional capacity, if you find yourself in situations that require you to work hard to achieve well, you may doubt whether you were meant to be in that situation/ relationship/ job role in the first place and you may even end up leaving because of your doubt.

Because of this, you may also allow yourself to be passed over for promotions thinking if it isn't easy for you, it isn't right.

The Superwoman[4]

The Superwoman thrives on being seen as a hard worker and being all things to all people. They define success as juggling all they have on their plates with excellence and ease. Failure for them means falling short of balancing all their roles and responsibilities well. Sound like the Strong Black Woman trope to you? Well, you're not wrong - more on that later.

This Impostor Type correlates well with Clance's core Impostor symptom of *'the superman/ superwoman aspects'* as both the symptom and the type are identified by the need for flawless performance in every part of life.

As a Superwoman, you have set very high standards for yourself in every area of responsibility out of a fear that you don't measure up with everyone around you.

So even if you are doing well as a parent or partner at the moment, meanwhile you are struggling with work or vice versa you feel like an all-around failure.

Unless you are working hard in every area of your life, you don't feel you are worthy of your success. Relaxation is almost a curse word to you, as you believe validation only comes through working hard.

At work, you often stay late to get a jump start on tomorrow's tasks before you dash home to bake the cake your child needs to take to the school bake. Buying a cake on the way home from work is an insult to you. Hobbies are a luxury you don't have time for between work AND family responsibilities AND charity work.

The Soloist

The Soloist thrives on being able to achieve great things by themselves. DIY is their motto and with enough time and effort they think they can become completely 'self-made'. Social Media has elevated being self-made to another level of attraction to many people. However, caution is required to not let illusions of being self-made created by some influencers become your measure of what's real and what's possible.

Soloists define success as anything achieved independently, therefore asking for or needing help is a sign of failure to them.

As a Soloist, you prefer to work on your own, because you believe if you were really competent, you wouldn't need help. If you have to ask for help, or if it is given to you within the context of teamwork for example, you feel like a fraud attributing any sense of achievement to yourself. Deep down you may find group work a nightmare and judge those who ask for help as incompetent.

You might end up unknowingly overburdened because you assume you should be able to complete all the work you were given, when it was actually work for more than one person.

***

Any of the above types sound familiar to you? Or familiar to the significant people in your life? You might see yourself or them in more than one of the types which is fine too. In addition, the types may also show up situation specific, but you might recognise a dominant one for yourself.

My dominant Impostor Type is The Expert and I'll be discussing its repercussions for my life in a few chapters. If you haven't taken the quiz yet and would like to know your type, here's the link: **https://blueprintway.com/is-quiz/**

“

If our caregivers provided us with a secure base to roam the world from as children, where mistakes were allowed and even encouraged for the sake of exploration and creativity, and if they were appropriately meeting our needs, we are likely to develop a secure attachment style as adults.

”

Impostor Types and Attachment Styles

The psychological concept of attachment styles posits that a person's early relationships with their caregivers strongly affect how they relate to others as an adult [5].

If our caregivers provided us with a secure base to roam the world from as children, where mistakes were allowed and even encouraged for the sake of exploration and creativity, and if they were appropriately meeting our needs, we are likely to develop a secure attachment style as adults.

However, if we lack that secure attachment as children, we may become adults who are either anxious, avoidant or a mix of both (known as disorganised) in the way we engage with the world.

Our attachment styles shape how we think, how we perceive and how we relate to the world around us[6].

Although Young's Impostor Types are not based on psychological research, they map well with two of the insecure attachment styles.

I propose that all Impostor Types, bar The Soloist, correlate with the anxious attachment style in that they are compelled to perform at a certain standard, for fear of being abandoned if they don't.

The Perfectionist fears being rejected if they don't perform perfectly; The Expert if they don't know all things; The Superwoman if she doesn't live up to the image of the Strong Black Woman/ Hero/ Selfless Saviour; and The Natural Genius if they don't create first attempt masterpieces.

The Soloist is an outlier here because they actually distance themselves from others, which would correlate better with the avoidant attachment style. They may avoid exposing their vulnerabilities by asking others for help, because it may have cost them dearly in the past. Instead, to protect themselves, they might become emotionally unavailable and extremely independent.

With that in mind, as we explore how to leverage our Impostor Types for our benefit in the next chapter, an important first step for all Impostor Types is the need to make ourselves feel more secure. This is both secure in ourselves, as well as more securely attached to others. More on that later.

Key Ideas

- Valerie Young identified 5 Impostor subtypes
    - **The Perfectionist:** feels like a fraud if they can't do things perfectly
    - **The Expert:** feels like a fraud if they lack knowledge/ qualifications in an area
    - **The Natural Genius:** feels like a fraud if they don't succeed with ease on the 1st try
    - **The Superwoman:** feels like a fraud if they can't juggle all their responsibilities flawlessly
    - **The Soloist:** feels like a fraud if they can't achieve success on their own
- There may be a correlation between some insecure attachment styles and the Impostor Types
- Core to challenging all Impostor Types is rebuilding our sense of safety and security

Endnotes

1 Young (2011)

2 Micromanage: desire to control every detail of an activity leading to exact instructions for the person executing them and scrutinising whether the instructions are followed

3 Sakulku & Alexander (2011)

4 I will be using the term superwoman as a default moving forward, but feel free to apply Superhero/Superman/ Superstudent/ Superperson to yourself if that feels more comfortable for you

5 Harlow (2021)

6 Harlow (2021)

CHAPTER 5

Impostor Subtypes Reframed

Contrary to Dr. Young, I don't think the different Impostor Types are *all* bad. In fact, I believe they can actually point us to a deeper sense of our purpose if we let them.

So, here are Dr. Young's subtypes with my added reframed (reconsidered) purpose and a proposal of first steps to take towards bossing your unique Impostor type.

From Perfectionist to Quality Assurance Specialist

Behind your drive for perfectionism is the desire to do things with excellence. You are a natural standard bearer. Quality assurance is in your DNA.

Instead of letting the chase for unattainable perfection drive you (and those around you) crazy:

1. ***Focus on progress first, perfection can be attempted later.*** Imperfect action beats perfect inaction every time. What's the first step you can take towards progress, even if it isn't perfect?

2. ***Set S.M.A.R.T. goals.***[1] 'Perfect' is not a specific, measurable, attainable, relevant, or time-bound standard. Let your KPIs (Key Performance Indicators) set the standard for you instead of a vague notion of perfectionism.

3. ***Delegate where possible.*** Actually, setting S.M.A.R.T. goals helps you trust others more in attaining the goal because they are no longer being measured against a subjective standard you don't even really understand. Instead, others have clear, specific instructions to follow.

4. ***Play more!***[2] Perfectionism stifles creativity, so get out of your head and do something fun for a while. Who knows, it might help with the problem at hand?!

5. ***Make templates.*** This is especially for those of us who deliberate forever over creating the perfect response to tasks that tend to repeat themselves in some shape or form. Instead of

spending time reinventing the wheel, if you've done a particular activity once and given your all for it and know it is great, use it as a template for all similar tasks - think emails, essay structures, project plans, client intake forms, budget templates etc.

The Perfectionist Impostor Type is one I struggled with primarily during my first term, in my first year of university. Having spent my formative years in the German educational system focusing more on exams than on essays, the switch to essay writing in English was more difficult for me than I initially cared to admit.

After receiving back my very first university essay grade in which I had barely scraped a pass mark, I used to let perfectionism paralyse me into procrastinating writing essays. This was because I falsely believed the only way to hand in a perfect essay, was to start writing it perfectly too.

I continued in this paralysis until one day, when I realised fretting over the perfect start to my essay was actually not bringing me any closer to having an essay at all, let alone a perfect one!

At that moment, the phrase *'progress first, perfection later'* dropped in my mind and it released me to just start, regardless of how terrible it would be to begin with.

And although I obviously never attained perfection, I ended up writing and eventually submitting essays that brought me high grades.

This consistency in turning in very good essays was because I eventually also started following Tip 5 of making templates. Once I had a couple of very good essays under my belt, I realised there was a pattern to structuring my essays, depending on what the instruction verb was i.e. 'evaluate', 'compare and contrast', 'analyse', 'discuss', 'examine' etc.

No matter the rest of the essay title, the instruction verb gave me a rough plan of how the essay needed to be structured. So, my task was then to research and find the missing puzzle pieces that would complete the big picture of my essay.

I can't tell you how satisfied I felt, no longer being paralysed by fear, but actually enjoying the puzzle creating process.

From Expert to Student Teacher

Behind your drive for expertise is a high value for wisdom and knowledge. You are a natural student. Being academic is in your DNA.

Instead of letting the chase for knowing it all drive you (and those around you) crazy:

1. ***Focus on what you already know first.*** Knowledge itself isn't power, applied knowledge is. What use is having all the degrees and not remembering what you learned?

2. ***Teach others what you know.*** The best way to retain what you've learned, deepen your understanding, and grow your confidence, is by teaching others about it. Use articles, videos, courses, speaking engagements etc. as your platform.

3. ***Make peace with 'Just in Time Learning'.*** You will never know everything, so why not embrace the fact that sometimes you just have to learn on the spot?

4. ***Niche down!*** The more specific your field of expertise is, the easier it is to know your field of expertise. No one can know everything and trying to chase knowledge in all will leave you a jack of all knowledge, master of none!

5. ***"I don't know"*** It's okay to admit when you don't know something. No one knows it all. Confess to the fact that you need to do some more research into a particular area if someone asks you a question about something you don't know - most people prefer an honest answer to a false one.

Padma Lakshmi, model, actress, TV host and author of several cookbooks once mentioned in an interview how Tip 1 of focusing on what she did know instead of what she didn't know, helped her work through her Impostor Syndrome while filming Season 1 of Top Chef many times.[3]

As mentioned, The Expert Impostor Type is my personal default self doubt flavour. I'd say it shouldn't be much of a surprise seeing I grew up surrounded by Black Intellectuals. Postgraduate study was a norm among the doctors, marine biologists, judges, solicitors and engineers I call family. Add to that, I genuinely love learning and reading and teaching.

So, the fact that I haven't got a Masters Degree, let alone a Doctorate is a source of Impostor Syndrome I have to deal with regularly.

Even as I write now, I have to fight to accept my current academic status and not to add a disclaimer to my previous sentence, for fear of you, the reader, looking down on me.

Instead, just as with Padma, focusing on what I already know has been a great first step towards bossing my Impostor Syndrome.

I'm the type of person who can get lost in a rabbit hole of journal article after journal article, book after book, all revealing more knowledge I have no clue about.

But instead of letting my natural love for learning push me over the edge into a black hole of never knowing enough, I now try to leverage what I already know more. Practically, it looks like writing and finishing a book on Impostor Syndrome even though I know I could continue writing, because there is so much more to say.

I also apply Tip 2 of teaching others what I already know, again through this book and also through workshops, webinars, speaking opportunities etc.

This has all happened because I chose to apply Tip 4 and niche down, not just on my target audience, but also on my topic.

It's much easier feeling confident about the understanding I have on how Impostor Syndrome affects women of colour, than on trying to feel confident about understanding mental health for all peoples and populations.

And finally, I'm learning to be more comfortable with not knowing, even if it is not knowing something about Impostor Syndrome and Black women, my niche.

After all, we Black women are not a monolith - ultimately, we are all unique in our perspectives, experiences and abilities. Also, I'm human, not God!

From Natural Genius to Person of Influence

Behind your drive for effortless expertise is a desire to do many things excellently. You are a natural leader. Talent is in your DNA.

Instead of letting the chase for first attempt masterpieces drive you (and those around you) crazy:

1. Remember that: ***'Hard work beats talent when talent doesn't work hard'*** - the greats in any sphere were not just made great by their talent, they worked hard to become great.

2. With so many things you are naturally good at, you can connect with many people and have great influence and even power. And ***with great power comes great responsibility.*** So, find out who/where/what you are called to lead and be diligent in your work.

3. Make peace with being a ***genius in progress***. Michelangelo once said: "Genius is eternal patience", meaning being a genius is more of a process than a destination. In addition, effortlessness does not inspire or truly motivate you or others; whereas working hard and seeing results does. It's the natural principle of reaping and sowing. You can truly enjoy what you know you worked hard to get.

4. ***Mind the gap.*** There is a journey between starting as a novice and becoming an expert that most people are familiar with, but it may seem like a foreign concept to the Natural Genius. If this is you, remember there is a process to all growth - roots can take a while to grow before shoots come up above ground.

Regardless of how you feel about the talents of the likes of Beyoncé or the late Kobe Bryant, it can never be said about them that they are/were lazy.

Many of us have come to appreciate their insane work ethic goes/went hand in hand with their natural talent.

I've identified The Natural Genius Impostor Type has cropped up in my life when I've started something that predominantly relies on skills I think I already have some level of maturity in - think studying, communicating and empathising. This has often led to me not minding the gap between the start and finish point in those situations.

So, when I went about completing the first draft of this book for example, I didn't doubt my writing ability at all, and felt fairly accomplished throughout the process.

That's because I was arrogantly relying on my academic and article writing skills as a gauge for how good my book writing skills would be. Needless to say, they are nowhere near the same!

My rude awakening came after bae[4] graciously chose to read my introduction and from the first sentence onwards listed a litany of recommendations to improve my writing.

Initially, I was inclined to ignore them all seeing that Gyles (my husband) isn't my target audience. But his suggestions did make me realise, I was expecting a near perfect first draft and my rising level of defensiveness wasn't because of him, but because I wanted to believe my writing needed little, to no help (hello Soloist tendencies, I see you too!).

The irony of it all was that Gyles's main feedback was that I was not taking up enough space in my book. It read like I was trying to rush people along to the main point - The F.R.A.U.D. Framework™

(which I was), while hurriedly and impatiently telling my own story of how I got there in the first place (which I was too).

In the reading of just one paragraph of my book, Gyles could sense my Impostor Syndrome of not feeling good enough and worthy enough of more of my readers' attention - yikes!

After some time away from writing, by the time I came back to work on the 2nd draft, I realised myself how good an effort draft 1 was, and yet how bad a final book it would have made.

I put in the consistent hard work of exploring more of what makes an effective self help book and how I could make it more personable, as well as put in the work of actually being disciplined in writing and revising the book.

Of course, the ultimate judge of the readability and usefulness of this book will be you, my reader, but now I can at least say I truly gave it my best, not my first.

From Superwoman to Queen of Boundaries

Behind your drive for multi-domain expertise is the desire to be validated and seen as trustworthy and reliable. You are a natural giver. Empathy is in your DNA.

Instead of letting the chase for external validation drive you (and those around you) crazy:

1. ***Reset your source of validation*** - hard work doesn't make you valuable. You are already inherently valuable. Build on strengthening your opinion of yourself. Don't let others tell you you aren't enough.

2. ***RELAX!*** You deserve a break. Workaholics don't have a good quality of life, so cut yourself some slack for not doing it all perfectly and breathe.

3. ***Self-care is not selfish!*** Focus on your needs too. You can't continually neglect your own needs and wants for the sake of working hard for others.

4. ***Make prioritising your superpower.*** Similar to the perfectionist, not everything and everyone requires you to bring your A game at all times. Who are the people and what are the things you should truly be prioritising? Not everything that is urgent is important and not everything that is important is urgent. Learning to prioritise is key.

Interestingly, after 300+ completions of my 'What's Your Impostor Type' quiz, The Superwoman subtype is the most prevalent result.

Almost one third of quiz completers have this as their top Impostor Type - the vast majority of them are women of colour.

I wonder, is it because we feel like we have to overcompensate all the time? Have our parents lovingly meant instructions of being "twice as good to get just as far" as our white peers got us to this place where failure is never an option for us?

Or is it maybe because we are trying to put to bed the racist stereotype of Black people being lazy and instead try to uphold the similarly destructive Strong Black Woman trope?

Or is it in light of 70% of single mothers juggling parenting and employment[5], their circumstances force them to be the Superwoman in their work and family?

Whatever the case may be, many of us seem to have a persistent struggle with equating our worth with our level of productivity.

That being said, I appreciate the tips above can only help so far. Trying to undo the trauma of centuries of intersectional oppression with a self-help hack is short-lived at best, and retraumatizing at worst. If you need more help than the tips can provide, please don't feel ashamed to reach out and ask for it.

From Soloist to Interdependent Adult

Behind your drive to DIY everything is the desire to be considered as competent solely on your own merit. You are a natural self-starter. Independence is in your DNA.

Instead of letting the chase for being completely self-made drive you (and those around you) crazy:

1. Remember that ***no man is an island*** - it can get lonely never asking for help.

2. Know that you can never detect your own ***blind spots*** yourself, so you limit your growth potential when you don't ask others for help.

3. Consider that asking for help isn't a sign of incompetence, but a sign of extending yourself beyond your current level of limitation. If we insist on doing everything ourselves, we end up ***limiting our potential.***

4. **Delegate** wherever and whenever you can as this allows you to focus on your zone of genius[6]. Dr. Valerie Young's rule of thumb is: "Assign a task to the lowest level in the organisation at which it can be performed competently"[7].

It is said that The Superwoman is The Perfectionist and Soloist on steroids so if you are one of the many who identifies with The Superwoman Impostor Type, you may want to pay attention to The Soloist tips too, and vice versa.

“

Learning about the subtypes was very eye-opening to me, because as a counsellor and coach the underlying problem I seem to be dealing with the most with my clients is a variation of Impostor Syndrome.

”

If asking for help is really hard for you, it may be because it was never modelled to you that asking for help is a safe and acceptable behaviour and that it doesn't reveal an unacceptable flaw in your character.

In this day and age, striving for independence is a virtue, so no wonder The Soloist can have a hard time recognising something isn't right in their definition of success being 'doing it by myself as often as possible' if much of the world is striving for the same.

But going through life DIYing everything can rob us of the opportunity to honour others and be honoured by others ourselves. I'll talk about this in more detail in the Reframing part of The F.R.A.U.D. Framework™.

Not asking for help can also limit our potential, as explained by Vygotsky's Zone of Proximal Development. Lev Vygotsky was a Soviet psychologist who reasoned that learning relies heavily on social interactions with official or unofficial teachers and that to grow our potential we have to interact with others[8].

Our Zone of Proximal Development describes the learning we can do with the help of others' guidance. Instead, if we choose to always walk alone, we end up victim to our own blindspots and biases.

If you are The Soloist and in a management position it is imperative to learn to delegate according to the rule of thumb mentioned above. Maybe there are genuinely things only you can do and have to do by yourself, but it can't be everything, or else you probably don't need a team around you.

This is a lesson I'm glad I learned early in my management role, or else I would have burned out much sooner than I eventually did.

Learning about the subtypes was very eye-opening to me, because as a counsellor and coach the underlying problem I seem to be dealing with the most with my clients is a variation of Impostor Syndrome.

Whether it is dressed in feelings of shame and inadequacy, anxiety, depression, perfectionism, procrastination, repressed emotions, they often lead back to a fractured relationship with ourselves (inadequacy), with our standards (incompetency), and with others (isolation).

Key Ideas

- I propose we can reframe Young's Impostor Types for our benefit
- There is a way to reframe each subtype to recognise its strengths and mitigate for weaknesses
- A set of action steps are proposed to start the reframing process
    - From Perfectionist to Quality Assurance Specialist
    - From Expert to Student Teacher
    - From Natural Genius to Person of Influence
    - From Superwoman to Queen of Boundaries
    - From Soloist to Interdependent Adult
- Many challenges we face could be down to underlying fears of inadequacy, incompetence and isolation

Endnotes

1 A goal many of us may relate to is the goal of being more active. Making the goal S.M.A.R.T. means making it specific, measurable, attainable, relevant and time-bound. The S.M.A.R.T. goal of being more active sounds something like 'Walk 30 minutes a day, 5 days a week, by 1 month from now' - it's very specific in what needs to be done; we can measure 30 minutes and if it is done 5 days a week; it is attainable to spare 30 minutes a day for a walk, even if it is broken down into 3x 10 minute slots, or 2x15 minutes; the goal is relevant to valuing a more active lifestyle and better long-term health; and it is time-bound by the fact this goal needs to be achieved within the next 4 weeks

2 Research shows that play for adults can help relieve stress, boost creativity, improve social and problem-solving skills and promote emotional well-being cp.https://www.helpguide.org/articles/mental-health/benefits-of-play-for-adults.htm

3 Simon (2017)

4 Bae (Before anyone else): affectionate term often used to describe one's significant other

5 Single Parents on Holiday (2020)

6 Zone of Genius: the area in which your passions and strengths overlap leading you to provide consistently great results for yourself and others

7 Young (2011) p.128

8 Open University (2019)

CHAPTER 6

Impostor Subtypes and Procrastination

During a Q&A session in my 'Interrupt Your Impostor Type' Workshop in May 2021, the question of how to deal with procrastination came up.

As I reflected further on the question, I realised depending on our Impostor Type, we may procrastinate in different ways, requiring different approaches to resolving procrastination. I'll be speaking about how these different ways of procrastinating are embodied through 4 different Procrastinator Types below.

To note, this chapter isn't here to judge you, but to invite you to reflect on what procrastination might actually be costing you. You may have different reasons to procrastinate, whether it is one of the four mentioned below or not. No matter your reason, know that there is a consequence – it's up to you to decide whether you can live with it or not. If you'd like to talk it through with a coach or counsellor, feel free to book a free consultation call with me.

Defining Procrastination

Although many of us are all too familiar with the topic of procrastination, this is the definition I'll be working from for the rest of this chapter:

"Procrastination is the act of consistently and unnecessarily delaying or postponing what we believe we should be doing now"

This definition therefore excludes things we don't deem as important enough to do any time soon, as well as the fact that emergency situations can necessarily interrupt our plans.

When I talk about procrastination, I mean that although we have identified tasks as important and there seems to be no logical explanation for why we are not doing them, it has become a pattern of behaviour to not do them.

Now that we are clear on our working definition, let's get to know the 4 Procrastinator Types.

Type 1: The Hater

No matter who we are or what our Impostor Type is, we all come across the occasional task we absolutely hate or very much dislike doing (cleaning out the drain comes to mind for me!).

If you are faced with such tasks all the time, you might want to spend time reflecting on your lifestyle. If your life consists of constant hard slug tasks, there may be a bigger matter to address and coaching, counselling or therapy could help with that.

If, however, you mostly love your life, the tasks that are your responsibility are mostly acceptable and there are only a few dislikes here and there, then the next four ideas are for you.

1. ***Delegate*** – If you can, see if you can delegate the task to someone else. Ideally someone who can complete it competently and doesn't hate it as much as you. But bear in mind, unless you are hiring their services, to be fair, be willing to take on tasks from them that they may want to delegate from time to time too.

2. ***Sweeten the deal*** – find a way to combine what you have to do but hate doing with something you love to do e.g., if you hate doing dishes, do it while you are catching up with a friend over the phone.

   Or, complete that really boring admin task, while listening to music you enjoy that isn't distracting. Remember though that only certain tasks can truly be multitasked, so if your hated task isn't one of them, this idea might not be for you.

3. ***Reward your effort*** – if it is a task that can't be multitasked with another task, give yourself something to really look forward to after having completed your task instead. That way there is a happy ending associated with completion of it, even if the rest of the process was not happy at all.

4. ***Just do it*** – in the words of Nike, sometimes, we just need to suck it up and get it done. The dread of doing the task often exaggerates how bad the task actually is. Remember, the sooner you start, the sooner you can finish.

Type 2: The Overwhelmed

This Procrastinator Type is strongly linked with The Superwoman and The Soloist Impostor Types. That's because this type of procrastination has to do with having too much on your plate for one person, something The Superwoman and The Soloist know all too well.

Overwhelm can keep you in a state of consistent low-level anxiety which activates your flight or freeze responses. So, you may be procrastinating because everything is a little bit too much for you at the moment.

Here are some ideas that might help if you resonate with this type:

1. ***Get grounded*** – if you are experiencing low level anxiety, it's important to re-establish your sense of psychological safety. This can happen through grounding activities that calm down your heightened nervous system, such as deep breaths, muscle relaxation, meditation, and mindfulness. Or you may want to consider counselling or therapy.

2. ***Take a break*** – sometimes the best thing you can do to deal with overwhelm is to stop and take a break. Have a nap, focus on self-care, plan something fun for yourself. It's hard to problem solve when you feel frazzled, so try and take some time out if you are feeling worn out. Your mental health deserves looking after.

3. ***Prioritise*** – one of the main reasons this type feels overwhelmed is because they don't know where to start. Everything seems urgent, and everything seems important. But the first step to stop procrastinating is to figure out what

the real priorities are and work through them, one at a time. A prioritisation tool that can help, is the Eisenhower Matrix, also known as the Urgent/Important Grid.

4. ***Delegate*** – The Superwoman and Soloist find it hard to ask for help as their sense of competence is tied to being capable based on their own merit. Yet, part of prioritising is also identifying what can be delegated to someone else. Are there things overwhelming you that you can outsource to someone else? If yes, see this act of delegation like a mental declutter or detox that will free up your capacity to act on the tasks you can't or don't want to delegate.

Type 3: The Thinker

This Procrastinator Type is primarily associated with The Expert and The Perfectionist Impostor Types. That's because this type of procrastination has to do with working out what needs to be done on a logical and intellectual level first. Reflection is the focus, because imperfect or ignorant action is to be avoided.

It's not a problem making contemplation a step towards completion of your task, but if you end up spending most of your time contemplating and not acting, you might be suffering from analysis paralysis – the occurrence when you over analyse and overthink a situation, to the point you can't make a decision, for fear of making the wrong decision.

Here are a few proposals to help you get unstuck:

1. ***Progress first, perfection later*** – try and take a first step, no matter how small, towards completing the task you've been procrastinating. You can always go back and change it later, but unless your task affects life or death situations, imperfect action beats perfect inaction every time.

   See it as an experiment or as a design process; start with something and as you inform yourself more and think about it more, it goes through different experimental cycles or design iterations.

2. ***Write it down*** – just the process of writing your reflections on your task down can lead to new insights you wouldn't have achieved if it's all still in your head. This is why journalling is such a powertool for mental health. Being able to look at what you were thinking about written down can not only stimulate your brain in a different way, it can also free up

energy spent on trying to remember it all without a memory aid. As the saying goes: "Paper never forgets".

Just don't lose the paper.

3. ***Talk it through*** – I know this one can seem especially daunting for those of us who don't want to share anything with others until we find it perfect. But explaining your approach towards completing your task to someone else can also lead to further insights on how to complete it more efficiently and effectively, based on their insight.

   Whether it is your manager, your colleagues, your family or your friends, their perspectives may highlight blind spots in your approach or provide validation for your approach.

   So why not plan a chat with someone who can give you informed feedback?

4. ***Know the S.M.A.R.T. Goal*** – One of the issues for both The Expert and The Perfectionist Impostor Types is that they both aspire towards achieving an impossible standard of success – one is Omniscience, the other is Perfectionism.

   With such lofty goals to work towards, no wonder we might put off getting started and instead try to figure things out mentally first! But without goals that are S.M.A.R.T. (specific, measurable, achievable, realistic and time bound) we set ourselves up for disappointment.

   Instead, look at the task you are procrastinating on and identify what successful completion of that task would look like expressed as a S.M.A.R.T. goal. Being able to quantify success can make aspiring towards it much easier.

Type 4: The Non-Committer

The final Procrastinator Type is strongly linked with the Natural Genius Impostor Type. That's because this type of procrastination has to do with 'Shiny Object Syndrome' – the desire to follow or be distracted by the next cool idea or new task, therefore not committing to the necessary task at hand.

This means you are really motivated to start something new but procrastinate on completing tasks that don't seem as 'sexy' as the new thing that's come around. You may start a million new projects, because you enjoy applying your competence to a new challenge and completing it effortlessly.

As an entrepreneur, visionary or creative, ideation is a desired trait, so this is often not seen as a problem. However, the problem with this Procrastinator Type is that you likely don't follow through and finish projects, either leaving others to pick up your slack or you are left with many great ideas, but no actions to show for them.

If you are putting off doing work because of this, hopefully the following proposals can help:

1. ***Think Big Picture*** – having wrestled with this Procrastinator Type myself most recently, I completely get the allure of wanting to go after the next cool and exciting task. After all, you are already motivated to do it and your creative juices are high.

   But it is important to remind yourself of the vision you are working towards and how the tasks you need to complete fit into that. Yes, they might not sound sexy or look shiny right now, but if they are ultimately going to lead to your vision being fulfilled, they are really important to stick to.

“

Our Impostor subtype may influence a multitude of our behaviours including how we procrastinate

”

2. ***Avoid Comparison*** – we've heard it before *"Comparison is the thief of joy"*. As a Natural Genius it is already a task to regulate your desire for new challenges and new ways to prove your competence.

   Adding comparison to that is like adding fuel to a fire. Unless your task is related to doing a competitor analysis, avoid comparing yourself to others, and instead focus on just doing you. Or else, you'll end up pursuing someone else's vision by copying the tasks they are completing.

3. ***Embrace the process*** – Ideas are seeds and for them to really flourish into success, they require time, work, and resources. Yes, new ideas are cool, but mature ideas can give you that sustainable success most of us are really after. So, embrace the fact that committing to completing a task will, in the long run, yield higher results, than constantly starting something new.

4. ***Hire a team*** – I'm all for locking into your unique zone of genius and not trying to be jack of all trades. So, if your strengths primarily lie in envisioning successful ideas and letting others work them out to completion, then hire a team around you that can take the baton you pass them and make something solid out of it. Of course, it will cost you money and time to do that, but the benefit is it's much less likely you'll have to work on anything that you're not excited about again.

Key Ideas

- Our Impostor subtype may influence a multitude of our behaviours including how we procrastinate
- I propose 4 Procrastinator Types and how they related to the Impostor Types
    - **The Hater:** the task at hand is not enjoyable at all - relatable to all Impostor Types
    - **The Overwhelmed:** the task at hand is too much to manage - especially resonates with The Superwoman and The Soloist
    - **The Thinker:** fear of the task leads to analysis paralysis in starting it - especially resonates with The Perfectionist and The Expert
    - **The Non-Committer:** the task is not as exciting as the next cool idea - especially resonates with The Natural Genius
- There are actions to take to stop procrastinating with each type

CHAPTER 7

Impostor Exotypes

Origins

One thing I've noticed since running workshops on Bossing Your Impostor Syndrome, working with clients exploring Impostor Syndrome 1:1, and even just in personal conversations - Dr. Young's subtypes can be confused to seem more related to an individual's personality and character traits, and not as much to the impact of the environment as a trigger for Impostor Syndrome.

Yet, research has shown that how much or how little in control of our environment we feel is a significant predictor of Impostor Syndrome[1].

And with the systemic oppressive impact society and institutions can have on people, most clearly seen in racism, sexism, genderism etc. I couldn't let the story of Impostor Syndrome seem most like an individual's or their immediate family's fault either.

Hence why I defined 4 Impostor Exotypes which are primarily based on how the external (Greek: 'exo') environment and socialisation causes, defines, and perceives our Impostor identity.

“

Research has shown that how much or how little in control of our environment we feel is a significant predictor of Impostor Syndrome.

”

Once again, I will add a content warning here to say that some of what is to come might be distressing to you. Please check in with yourself to identify if any of what you are reading is becoming too much for you to process right now or on your own.

Especially as we delve into topics of oppression and abuse, feel free to skip this chapter if you don't want to read about these topics. If you decide to continue reading, as a reminder if you feel triggered, consider taking a break and engaging in self-soothing or mindfulness activities such as deep breathing exercises, progressive muscle relaxation, listening to calming music, speaking to a trusted friend, seeking counselling etc.

Without further ado, these four Impostor Exotypes are:

- The Alien
- The Clone
- The Abused[2] and
- The Co-dependent[3]

The labels are intentionally negative because of how we are made to feel by our environment.

The Alien

The Alien finds themselves in settings where they are all too often made to feel like the odd-one-out, the foreigner, the black sheep. What has been declared as the standard or the norm looks, feels, sounds, nothing like them.

Black, Indigenous People of Colour (BIPOC) experience it all the time; women often too, but men can also experience this Impostor type in women-dominated fields like nursing, care work or homemaking.

So, you are left with a persistent, nagging feeling like you don't belong and that you are a fraud, regardless of whether you are actually achieving success in your context.

I've spoken about the realities of being a person of colour in the academic and corporate world in a previous chapter and all these experiences point to being typecast as an outsider who doesn't belong in the arenas of success we want to be in.

The perpetuation of microaggressions contribute to us feeling like we are illegal immigrants in a space we're not really welcome in.

In a book tour interview (My Forever) First Lady Michelle Obama opened up to students at a London school about the fact that her school guidance counsellor once told her she wasn't "Princeton material".

She went on to say:

"I still remember that feeling of doubt, that feeling of another adult placing a barrier on me that I didn't even have for myself. The person whose job it was to help young people reach their dreams, she saw me and whatever she saw in me told me that my dreams were too high."[4]

Thankfully Mrs. Obama superseded her guidance counsellor's low expectations of her and eventually did go to Princeton, but this sense of not belonging and feeling like she wasn't good enough, stayed with her for many years.

And this once again shows the danger of not appropriately highlighting how impactful our environment can be on us developing Impostor Syndrome.

As Mrs. Obama mentioned in her quote, she didn't even have Impostor Syndrome about attending an Ivy League school, she was courageous to dream big, despite her background being different. It was her school guidance counsellor who planted that seed within her that she wasn't good enough.

Many of us may have people around us who make us doubt ourselves, even in the moments when we do feel confident. Imagine if Mrs O had let that seed of external doubt grow, we may have never gotten to know and be inspired by her. And what about you? Who would you be if you never let the seeds of doubt others sow in you grow?

The Clone

The Clone finds themselves in settings where they are all too often made to feel like they are nothing special and everyone is just the same. What has been declared as the standard or the norm looks, feels, sounds, exactly like them and/or a better version of them.

They struggle with feeling special/significant because what was/could be their Unique Selling Point[5] in another context is a common trait in the context they are in now. So, you are left with a persistent, nagging feeling like you're just a small fish in a small pond and that you are a fraud for not being different enough or aspiring even higher.

It's akin to Clance's Impostor symptom of '*the need to be special, to be the very best*'. Having been socialised to stand out in their competencies, The Clone can then find it especially hard to blend in.

A clear example that comes to mind for me here is a trip I once took to visit a friend of mine living in Dublin and working at Google at the time. One evening, we went to dinner with a group of her Google colleagues and other friends of my friend.

Before that dinner, I spent most of my life feeling like an Alien – the only Black girl in my school in Germany, and then the only Black German at my university in the UK. I had gotten used to being the odd one out and even started enjoying and leveraging the 'special status' it afforded me (more on that later).

But at this Dublin dinner, I increasingly started feeling like a clone as I recognised very similar elements of my story of successfully leveraging my difference in person after person I spoke to.

And as the evening continued, I went from feeling like a clone ("we all speak at least two languages and have lived on two continents") to an outdated version of an expat clone when suddenly everyone else spoke at least 3 languages and had lived on at least 3 continents.

To clarify, people were not going around bragging, instead we were just sharing parts of our life story with each other. I just ended up feeling like I had drawn the short straw when it came to unique life experiences.

So, I left that dinner wondering if being typecast by my usual environment as The Alien for so long had lowered my ambitions to the point I'd actually become a fraud in the very lifestyle (being a bi-lingual expat) I held dear at the time.

The Abused

The Abused finds themselves in settings where they are actively oppressed or discriminated against. As one who is abused, no matter what you do, it never seems good enough to your abuser, and any success you have is minimised and disregarded.

So, you are left with a persistent, nagging feeling like you amount to nothing and that you are a fraud for working towards being in a better place than you currently are.

This is a phenomenon I have often witnessed in my work with survivors of sexual abuse. Although the abuse wasn't their fault (FYI, it is never the victim's fault!) it changes how they see themselves and they believe they must not be valuable or have worth for the abuse to have happened to them in the first place.

Transforming their lives then feels like a betrayal to the worthless person they were made to believe they really are. They feel like a fraud when trying to better their lives. If you resonate with the above - some of those thoughts need to be challenged (more on that later).

The Codependent

The Codependent finds themselves in settings where they are all too often made to feel like they are not capable of caring for themselves.

Codependency is still a form of abuse, but often socially more accepted, as in the case of helicopter parenting[6] even with adult children. As one who is co-dependent, you never really get to make decisions for yourself because the authority figure in your life wants to keep you dependent on them.

So, 'for the sake of your safety' or other reasons they come up with, these authority figures try to regulate your life.

This leaves you with a persistent, nagging feeling like you're not capable of doing anything for yourself and you think you are a fraud just considering independence.

Having spoken about this Impostor Type in my workshops, I remember two distinct responses to The Codependent type.

One was from a man who suddenly recognised how his parent's way of raising him had an impact on why he struggles with trusting his own voice as an adult now. The other response was from a mum to an adult who realised she needed to stop smothering her daughter or risk her remaining codependent.

I like how the alternate perspective of both examples shows that in many cases, the authority figure isn't trying to be abusive and even has good intentions, but it can still have real, detrimental effects on the individual.

This codependent dynamic can also play itself out in the work context. If you have a boss who micromanages you for no good reason, you may end up questioning your own ability and eventually think you can't be trusted without their guidance.

Or you may never accept your own ability in the first place, because you are trained to just carry out someone else's plans, and leave the thinking and creativity to them.

Do any of the above sound familiar to you?

Since I defined these types and started speaking about and teaching them in my workshops, there hasn't been one participant that couldn't resonate with at least one of the exotypes just as strongly, if not more than Dr. Young's subtypes.

In fact, most people I've spoken to about both types find themselves at an intersection of Impostor subtypes and Exotypes which shows me the Exotypes are a necessary contribution to the body of Impostor Syndrome research already out there.

Key Ideas

- Impostor Exotypes focus on how our environment can affect how we see ourselves as Impostors
- I propose 4 Impostor Exotypes that further explain this influence
    - **The Alien:** we are made to feel like the odd one out
    - **The Clone:** we are made to feel like the outdated model
    - **The Abused:** we are made to feel worthless
    - **The Codependent:** we are made to feel incapable of caring for ourselves

Endnotes

1 Peteet et al. (2015)

2 This type in particular comes with a content warning, due to sensitive topics

3 Codependency here is not due to addiction, but the overprotection of the caregiver

4 Biddlecombe, n.d.

5 Unique Selling Point: a distinguishing aspect of a product or service that makes it more appealing than its peers

6 Helicopter Parenting: hovering over every single detail of your child's life for the sake of protecting from all harm and promoting them towards success

CHAPTER 8

Impostor Exotypes Reframed

Despite the very negative labelling and experiences that were just described, I once again believe there is a positive, reframed purpose for each Impostor Exotype. I have described them and the proposed plans for shifting from the problem to the positive purpose below.

Disclaimer

However, as a major disclaimer - these reframed types point to leadership positions set out to engage with and change culture - something that can feel like a lot of unwanted pressure for some.

As one lady in my Interrupt Your Impostor Type workshop pointed out after discussing the reframed types, she wants to have 'permission to just be average', whereas the reframed types point more to the narrative of respectively being or becoming 'the model minority' or 'the model majority'.

I definitely hold my hand up to how my upbringing as a 'model minority'[1] in Germany, both based on my race and my faith, is part of what makes many of my strategies by default appeal to being or becoming the bigger and better person through leadership.

So, if any of what follows is too much for you, please do not take it on, don't burden yourself. But if you feel called to provoke change in your sphere or are just interested in what it might look like, read on.

"

By psychological safe space I mean a place where you feel like you belong, where you won't be judged or cancelled for asking questions, presenting ideas or challenging the status quo.

A place where you will be accepted, respected and valued.

"

Your psychological safe space

Now that you've decided to read on, I would be remiss if I did not strongly encourage you to only proceed with actioning the following steps if you already have a psychological safe space in your life.

By psychological safe space I mean a place where you feel like you belong, where you won't be judged or cancelled for asking questions, presenting ideas or challenging the status quo.

A place where you will be accepted, respected and valued.

I'm not only talking about a physical location, but a person/ group of people you can feel safe with. This can often be your family and friends, but it can also be a mentor, coach or counsellor.

The reason it is important to establish your safe space before attempting to make the changes below, is because change is costly and can be exhausting and heart-breaking, especially change that requires standing against current societal and institutional norms.

For example, if your workplace is the place that traumatises and makes you feel like an Impostor the most, challenging the status quo can end up with you being perceived as a threat which could cut you off socially and potentially even cost you your job.

It's imperative that you have people around you at such a time, who remind you that you are not the 'crazy' one, or that you are not being 'overly sensitive'. Instead, what makes these people your safe space is the fact that they can affirm the injustice you are suffering and remind you that "it's not you, it is definitely them" with the problem.

If you have someone in mind, as you read on, think of how they could help you reinforce the change you desire.

If you don't, why not contact a counsellor or therapist to be that touchpoint for you?

Counselling aka talking therapy enables you to develop a therapeutic alliance[2], or cooperative working relationship with a trained professional built on empathy, acceptance and confidentiality.

In a way, the therapeutic alliance between you and your counsellor/therapist is a professional stand-in for the secure attachments you may have missed out on in your past or are missing out on in your present.

The alliance provides you with a safe space and secure base from which to explore and engage with your internal and external world until you are able to create that safe space within your internal and external world.

From Alien to Ambassador

You are not meant to be an alien; you are an ambassador in the making. You are the first of your kind in a world desperately needing more of you. Your mere presence is forcing people to consider what they thought was 'normal' as an outdated, discriminatory concept.

Instead of letting the fact that you don't feel like you fit in drive you into isolation:

1. ***Embrace & Protect your difference.*** You are the only one who can master being you and if people are refusing to allow you to do so, it might be time to pack up and leave. The amount of safe spaces truly embracing diversity, equity and inclusion are thankfully growing around the world.

2. ***Celebrate your difference.*** This is your secret sauce, not a cause for concern. Don't let the ignorance of others, snuff out the joy of your heritage. Once again, more and more on-and off-line communities are creating safe spaces to celebrate your authentic self.

3. ***Share your difference.*** There is power in diversity so consider and build on the benefit of your personal point of view and skill set to your employer or company. As 'The Millionaire Maker' Danielle Leslie would ask *"what's your unique 'culture add'?"* [3]. Identify it and let it profit you and the businesses willing to support you in expressing it.

There are tons of examples of alien to ambassador transformations in the world! You really don't have to look too far to come across them.

If you still feel stuck, just look at almost any Black woman of fame/influence/success in a usually 'non-Black context' (pretty much every context) who hasn't tried to or let others force them to 'white-wash'/water down their identity and heritage.

Or research successful women in male-dominated fields who haven't dialled down or sacrificed their personal femininity to blend in better or be more accepted.

Some of the examples that come to mind for me are Michelle Obama, Oprah, Michaela Coel, Estelle, Bozoma Saint John, Gina Yashere, Yvonne Orji, Issa Rae, Malorie Blackman, Ruth E. Carter, Vice President Kamala Harris, Diane Abbott, Ava DuVernay, Misty Copeland - and the list goes on.

That certainly doesn't mean the Alien to Ambassador transformation is easy - I applaud all who are able to just be themselves in the face of opposition. It requires a special dose of courage not all of us immediately acquire, and that's okay.

If you are not able or willing to take on the ambassador role, but don't want to bear the emotional burden of being an alien, watch out for tips in the 'Defence' Step of The F.R.A.U.D. Framework™.

And if you are The Alien who finds themselves abused because of their diversity, being an Ambassador won't help. Remember, at the first sign of any violence committed against real life political ambassadors, they are evacuated to their country of origin. So please don't feel like you have to stand your ground as an Ambassador. Instead, the reframed version of The Abused Impostor Type might be more appropriate for you then.

From Clone to Architect

You are not meant to be a clone; you are an architect in the making. Your ability to effortlessly fit into the dominant culture enables you to develop blueprints of what works and what is sustainable for the average person around you.

If you are someone who is widely known, liked, and trusted in your context, you can also advise on any necessary, but hard changes to be made in a gentle and non-threatening way. This makes you a great ally for societal changes.

Instead of letting the fact that you don't feel like you stand out enough drive you to depression:

1. ***Embrace your context.*** Unless you know you should be going somewhere else, make peace with where you are at and be grateful for the stability and sense of belonging you've experienced so far.

2. ***Decode your context.*** Based on your perspective, you can identify standard practises in your context in case they need replicating somewhere else.

3. ***Improve your context.*** Recognise areas of improvement that are necessary within your context and advocate for them.

What this practically means for me is, instead of spending the Dublin Dinner becoming more doubtful of myself, I could have leveraged the opportunity to ask how other people managed the constant change in their lives; how they regularly connected with other like-minded people; how it affected their romantic relationships etc.

I was literally a bilingual expat sitting at a table of multilingual expats. Now I know, I could have listened and learned more for myself and also for the sake of being able to decode multilingual expat life for those who are interested in entering it but have no idea where to start.

As they say, hindsight is 20/20 - so I can't be mad I didn't see it then. But you can be mad at yourself if you've read, understood, and agree with this now and don't leverage the knowledge for when you find yourself in a similar context relevant to you.

The Clone to Architect transformation works really well whenever you find yourself as part of the majority culture in a certain context - one could say when you are with your tribe. And we all know that if we are only ever around those who look, sound, think, live like us, it is easy for stereotypes towards others, outside of our tribe, to fester.

This is why we are in a privileged position to advocate for positive change within our context when we are typecast as Clones. We can choose to be Architects of a new way of thinking, living, and sounding that is more diverse, inclusive and equitable.

Just because we may be women of colour, it doesn't mean we are never around people like us. It doesn't mean we are always The Alien. It doesn't mean we are always powerless. It doesn't mean we can't be bigoted towards people outside our in-group.

A quote that I love by author and activist Austin Channing-Brown states that:

"The work of anti-racism is becoming a better human to other humans".

Whenever I think of this quote, it makes me wonder, where do I and where does my tribe need to do more work in becoming a better human to other humans?

What are the challenging conversations that I as a Black woman need to have with other Black women in my tribe about being a better human to *all* humans?

What are the challenging conversations that I as a Christian need to have with other Christians in my tribe about being a better human to *all* humans?

What are the challenging conversations that I as a counsellor need to have with other counsellors in my tribe about being a better human to *all* humans?

What are the challenging conversations that I as a cis gender woman need to have with other cis gender women in my tribe about being a better human to *all* humans?

What are the challenging conversations that I as a 'Western World citizen' need to have with other 'Western World citizens' in my tribe about being a better human to *all* humans?

There is a level of influence I have in my tribe that an outsider won't. It's important I call out discrimination and inequality where I can in my tribes, so an outsider to those tribes doesn't think they have to do it. This could cause more pain than progress because they have no relationship in advance of their rebuke.

There is a level of influence you have in your tribe that an outsider won't. Figuring out your influence and leveraging necessary change is important to transition from Clone to Architect.

From Abused to Activist

I'm so sorry if you have been abused or are being abused, this is never acceptable and it is not your fault! You are not meant to be abused; you are an activist in the making. The unjust pain and abuse you have experienced are your fuel to change the world in such a way no one else needs to experience what you have.

As someone who knows what it feels like to be abused, you can relate to so many people in that space and encourage them to transform their lives too. Demanding change from oppressors by force is what you do through boycotts, protests, voting, lawsuits, voting with your money etc.

Instead of letting the fact that you've been abused drive you into vicious cycles of shame:

1. **Escape from your oppressors!** Abuse and discrimination are never acceptable, never!

   If you need help removing yourself from abusive or discriminatory situations, connect with your local helplines and support centres.

2. ***Empower yourself.*** Get a therapist or counsellor to help you work through the abuse and trauma in a gentle and safe way, so it is no longer holding you back.

3. ***Encourage others.*** If/when you feel ready, share your story with those you believe can benefit from it, who might have previously experienced or presently experience abuse.

The decision to transform from The Abused to The Activist is a highly personal one. It is entirely up to you if you ever feel like leveraging your story of abuse and survival for the benefit of helping others.

You choose if, when and who you share your story with. You may just want to focus on finding healing for yourself and leave it at that and that's not selfish.

From Codependent to Agent of Self Actualisation

You are not meant to be codependent; you are an Agent of Self-actualisation in the making. You are called to manage yourself well and be an example of self-agency to others. You are strong enough to be an interdependent adult, never codependent. You *can* make good decisions by yourself if you are willing to learn and put in the work to do so.

Instead of letting the fact that you don't feel like you can handle yourself lead you into reciprocated codependency:

1. ***Break away from your smotherers.*** Codependency is never healthy, never! It stifles both your and the other person's growth and potential.

2. ***Empower yourself.*** Get a therapist or counsellor to help you work through your codependency and mistrust of yourself in a gentle and safe way, so it is no longer holding you back.

3. ***Trust your voice.*** When you feel ready, start making decisions for yourself - from the simple, to the important ones.

Learning to trust ourselves and that the decisions we make are for our good is an important part of Adulting. Something I often see with people who have been in toxic relationships is their inability to trust their own choices again, because they blame themselves for the wrong relational choices they made in the past.

This is why counselling can be useful to evaluate all that contributed to those choices being made and coaching to practice making better choices for oneself.

Check in with yourself - how was all this for you?

Has this been a point of inspiration or frustration or both? Have some old wounds come up that you might want to address? If yes, take your time before you read on - process some of your thoughts and emotions through journalling, counselling or conversation with loved ones.

Key Ideas

- I propose we can reframe Impostor Exotypes for our benefit too
- It's important to create psychological safe spaces before engaging in the work of challenging the Impostor role society is pushing on you
- If we choose to accept the reframed purposes of the Exotypes, they provide steps towards the transformation of:
    - Alien to Ambassador;
    - Clone to Architect;
    - Abused to Activist;
    - Codependent to Agent of Self Actualisation

Endnotes

1 Model Minority: stereotypical view of a minority group as being more successful than other minority groups with the former being viewed as the ideal example of a minority

2 Therapeutic Alliance: cooperative working relationship with a trained professional built on empathy, acceptance and confidentiality

3 Leslie n.d.

CHAPTER 9

The F.R.A.U.D. Framework™

Introduction

Dr Young herself states: *"The goal is not to never feel like an impostor. The goal for me is to give [people] the tools and the insight and information to talk themselves down faster. They can still have an impostor moment, but not an impostor life."*[1]. I couldn't have said it better myself!

The research is clear - there is no magic one-time treatment for Impostor Syndrome, it can't be completely overcome, but that's okay. Because many successful people still live great lives despite having Impostor Syndrome.

The problems occur when we allow Impostor Syndrome to become a fixed identity rather than containing it as a temporary ideology. This can then stop us from progressing because we don't feel like we will ever be good enough.

“

Every expert started off as a student, so the world might miss out on your current and future expertise if you keep talking yourself up as an Impostor and down from doing what you are meant to do.

”

Yet, every expert started off as a student, so the world might miss out on your current and future expertise if you keep talking yourself up as an Impostor and down from doing what you are meant to do.

Bossing your Impostor Syndrome is not about being a perfectionist or being the best there ever was at [insert your job role of choice]. It's about learning to accept yourself - flaws and successes - and see the value you provide to your field and humankind, no matter what level of expertise you are at.

We cannot allow perfectionism and self-doubt to trap us in the most vicious of cycles in which we never feel good enough, but always aim to be perfect. This can cause serious anxiety and depression and negatively impact the quality of our lives.

Based on my analysis of Impostor Syndrome research and treatment options, I devised a 5-step framework for you to talk yourself down from self-triggered Impostor thoughts faster - I call it F.R.A.U.D. (see what I did there!?).

THE F.R.A.U.D. FRAMEWORK™ is a tool kit of evidence based techniques to improve your self compassion, self competence and social support, combating the feelings of inadequacy, incompetence and isolation Impostor Syndrome is known for.

Below is a figure of the 5 steps that can help you boss your Impostor Syndrome.

Figure 2: The F.R.A.U.D. Framework™

Although this is presented as a cyclical, progressive model, you might only need to work through one step before you can effectively challenge your thoughts and push past feelings of being an Impostor. The order is just there to help you remember each step better.

As you familiarise yourself with all the steps, there may be 1 or 2 that become your go-to solutions to boss your Impostor Type. So, let us have a look at these 5 steps in more detail.

Endnotes

1 Abrams (2018)

CHAPTER 10

F: Fact or Fiction?

"The only way to stop feeling like an impostor, is to stop thinking like an impostor."

DR VALERIE YOUNG

The principles of CBT

Impostor Syndrome is an issue that begins by occupying your thoughts, swiftly followed by your feelings which can then influence everything you do. Because the emotive side is so powerful, we can forget that our feelings don't just come out of nowhere. They are triggered by our thoughts.

Cognitive Behavioural Therapy or CBT is a psychological theory and approach that explores the connection between our thoughts, emotions, and behaviour. It is the most researched and scientifically supported psychological approach in mental health therapy[1].

CBT teaches us that:

1. Our thoughts are made up of our positive and negative core beliefs, assumptions, and automatic thoughts

2. Our feelings are based on our perceptions or thoughts of a particular situation, not the situation itself

3. Our behaviour is determined by our feelings

To change behaviour, we need to change feelings and to change feelings we need to change thoughts.

One side of tackling Impostor Syndrome requires us to examine our negative thoughts (also known as limiting beliefs or cognitive distortions[2]) and nip any falsehoods in the bud. Changing our thoughts is a matter of consistent, intentional practice, akin to changing our bodies in the gym.

This book and the psychological interventions presented are here to help you rewire your brain so that the negative no longer dominates your life and so that your internal Impostor narrative isn't just silenced but replaced by a better one.

It's about learning to choose the best thoughts which lead to better feelings and more confident behaviour.

“

To change behaviour, we need to change feelings and to change feelings we need to change thoughts.

”

Thought Trial Introduction

To change the Impostor narrative plaguing us, we need to put our thoughts on trial and identify and judge what is fact and what is fiction (hence the name of this step). To do that we need to collect the relevant pieces of hard, verifiable evidence and testimonials from others to help us piece things together.

Figure 3: Depiction of a Thought Trial

In life, we often just accept what the prosecutor (see Figure 3) tells us about our failures, fictitious information, and fraudulent behaviour, without questioning it.

But part of transforming our minds is to question the thoughts we have, especially those that keep us imprisoned in self-doubt and self-criticism.

The prosecutor is most likely you, but it can also be people whose opinion you care about, such as your parents or primary caregivers, authority figures in your life, colleagues, friends etc. Either way, you have either internalised their criticism of you or are vocally being criticised by them.

The main point of a prosecutor is to provide evidence that you committed a crime so you can be sentenced justly. In the case of Impostor Syndrome, your failures, fraudulent behaviours, and false information will be used as evidence against you, seeking to prove that you are a fraud.

Failures: lack of success in achieving something

Fraudulent behaviour: you are actually pretending to be someone you are not

Fictitious Information: Cognitive distortions

To boss your failures, you need to:

- accept you failed, but recognise you are NOT a failure
- learn from your mistakes
- recognise nobody is perfect and
- see it as a sign that you are trying to achieve something (more on that in the Reframing chapter).

To boss fraudulent behaviour just stop doing it. If you haven't achieved what you need in accredited professions, stop pretending you have and go do it if that's what you want to do.

But I'm begging you, please stop pretending to be a brain surgeon, an air traffic controller, a counsellor, a teacher, a lawyer, an accountant etc., if you haven't passed the relevant professional qualifications!

You should be feeling like a fraud all day, every day if you haven't!

If you haven't brought about significant results in an unaccredited field, start finding out how you can and deliver them. In the meantime, please stop pretending to be an experienced marketing exec, coach, manager, sales rep etc.

But if you work in a regulated field like medicine, teaching or counselling and you have passed the academic and practical parts, then you should be able to confidently say you do what you are trained to do.

Or, if you are working in an unregulated field like management, marketing, or coaching, then your ability to deliver the relevant results and your industry-relevant experience are more important than your qualifications.

If you are still feeling like an Impostor in both cases, I'm here to help you boss fictitious information. Because, to boss Fictitious information aka 'stinking thinking', you need to bring out your defendant.

The main point of a defendant is to provide evidence that you are not guilty of committing a crime, so you can be set free. In the case of Impostor Syndrome, your achievements, abilities, and accreditations will be used as evidence for your innocence of being a fraud.

Achievements: the results you provide

Abilities: your skills, strengths, talents

Accreditations: your externally assessed learning. It doesn't have to be a degree, but some structured learning that you have undertaken that is externally assessed in some way.

When setting up The Blueprint Way™, I had countless moments of Impostor Syndrome rearing its ugly head. Some days ended with me in tears, wanting to shut it all down, because I thought I wasn't qualified enough to run my own business.

And then one day, I was reviewing my CV and work experience for content for my website 'About' page and it suddenly hit me like a ton of bricks: no matter how strongly I felt like I wasn't good enough to start my business, my achievements told a very different story.

In that moment, I got such an incredible confidence boost, because I had years and years of evidence of achieving. Listing your achievements is a great way of tackling Impostor Syndrome by exposing it as a fictitious thought rather than a fact.

Reflection: Thought Trial

1. What area are you currently struggling the most with self-doubt in?

2. What objective evidence do you have for and against being an Impostor?

3. Based on the evidence, are you really guilty of being an Impostor or not?

If your verdict is that you are not guilty of being an Impostor and you are not committing fraudulent behaviour, I invite you to repeat the list of your achievements, abilities, and accreditations to yourself regularly from now on.

In this way, you reprogram your thoughts to readily recall your inner Defendant, instead of your inner Prosecutor. With consistent and intentional practice, your thoughts about yourself should start aligning with your facts and your feelings will eventually follow suit. If it's not working, remember there are 4 more steps to try out.

Specific Application

Although every section of The F.R.A.U.D. Framework™ is beneficial to all and any Impostor Types, there may be some sections that benefit some types the most.

The Fact or Fiction step is foundational to all types as every Impostor Type struggles in their own way with negative and limiting thoughts about their competence and achievements. Learning to challenge negative thoughts and putting them through a thought trial is therefore an essential skill for all.

A helping hand

If you are struggling to ask yourself these questions, or you need some accountability, or your verdict is that you indeed are a fraud, feel free to contact me, as some counselling or coaching might be of benefit to get more objective support.

Key Ideas

- To stop feeling like an Impostor, we need to stop thinking like one
- Feelings are not facts - they are clues to our thoughts
- Thoughts consist of our core beliefs, assumptions, and automatic thoughts
- Cognitive distortions are irrational beliefs we reinforce over time
- Putting our thoughts on trial is necessary to change our thinking

Endnotes

1 Ebb & Dobson (2010)

2 Cognitive Distortions: habitual thinking patterns that are mostly negative and inaccurate

CHAPTER 11

R: Reframing

"Our key to transforming anything lies in our ability to reframe it."

MARIANNE WILLIAMSON

Reframing is a psychological term referring to the ability to see a situation from a different perspective to our default one, to uncover a possible variety of different interpretations[1]. Reframing is another way of challenging our thoughts by applying a different filter (perspective), or by removing a bad filter (cognitive distortions), in real life.

We can often forget that we are not alone in our struggles. Every human deals with some Cognitive Distortions, but we often show what psychologists call 'pluralistic ignorance' - the false estimation that others don't believe the same thing we do[2].

When it comes to Impostor Syndrome, we automatically look at situations we face from a highly individual perspective, thinking we, as an individual, are a fraud, and we, as an individual, are not good enough and no one else feels this way, because no one else is a fraud.

I invite you to consider three other perspectives instead of pluralistic ignorance:

1. the *Humankind Perspective,*
2. the *Personal History Perspective, and*
3. *the Honour in Weakness Perspective.*

The Humankind Perspective

You are not alone in occasionally thinking that you are a fraud. As mentioned before, 70% of humanity has felt or will feel the same at one point in time[3]. Even the likes of Maya Angelou and Penélope Cruz have been known to feel like Impostors.

Maya Angelou, a civil rights activist, poet, memoirist, and actress, said of her own struggles with self-doubt:

"I have written eleven books, but each time I think, 'Uh oh, they're going to find out now. I've run a game on everybody and they're going to find me out'".

Meanwhile, Oscar winning actress Penélope Cruz has said of her struggles with Impostor Syndrome:

"I feel every time I'm making a movie, I feel like if it was my first movie. Every time I have the same fear that I'm gonna be fired. And I'm not joking. Every movie, the first week, I always feel that they could fire me!" [4].

Angelou and Cruz are not on their own in being high achievers with self-doubt.

If you google famous people with Impostor Syndrome further examples include Oprah, Tina Fey, Lupita Nyong'o, Tom Hanks, Ryan Reynolds, Tracee Ellis Ross, J Lo, and the amazing Michelle Obama to name just a few and the list goes on and on and on. So, I'd say we are in great company.

In fact, Tom Hanks, one of the most recognisable film stars in the world, once admitted:

"No matter what we've done, there comes a point where you think, 'How did I get here? When are they going to discover that I am, in fact, a fraud and take everything away from me?'" [5].

This goes to show no matter how much on top of your game you are, you can still feel like you're faking it. Doubt is a normal part of our humanity, but you cannot allow it to paralyse you.

Reflection: Impostor Role Models

1. Who are your biggest role models in the areas you feel most insecure in?

2. What journey and experiences with self-doubt have they had?

The Personal History Perspective

We've covered the fact that Impostor Syndrome has a lot to do with not feeling like we belong. We struggle to internalise our successes in our given field of practice, because we think we are not a valid or valuable member of that field.

This might be because of:

1. less experience due to newly qualifying
2. being of a different demographic in comparison to the dominant players or recognised experts in our chosen field (e.g., age, ethnicity, gender, disability, religion, sexuality etc.)
3. an unconventional training journey, maybe because of a career change
4. unusually rapid promotion/progress
5. having a different personality type (introvert, ambivert, extravert) or leadership style to the established ones in your environment

When Gyles (my husband) first started off in his chosen career as a Clinical User Experience (UX) Designer, he struggled with many moments of self-doubt, especially because he was the first to do so.

Leveraging his medical degree and training, he carved out his own path in the field of UX and is now an accomplished Clinical UX Designer, founder of the global Clinical UX Association and Academy, and a sought-after international speaker and conference host.

“

Your story is really about recognising and communicating your worth and value which can often be found in the things you have overcome or experienced - after all, diamonds are made through the pressure they endure.

”

All of this would have never happened, had he chosen to give in to self-doubt and abort his plans, or had he let perfectionism stop him from making any progress.

We all need to accept that our personal history is not the same as someone else's and that is not a weakness. In fact, it actually gives us a different vantage point which we can capitalise on as we develop our personal or professional brands. Whether you are an employee or entrepreneur, you need to learn to tell your unique story as it is core to selling yourself as a brand and therefore core to your salary negotiations or business profits.

When I started my entrepreneurial journey, hearing the phrase 'tell your story' made me break out in cold sweats, because not only did I not fully know what that meant, but I had also been clearly terrible at it in the recent past. As previously mentioned, I had failed to secure the same job I was already doing very well when I had to re-apply for it due to a department restructure and it was primarily down to me not telling my story and selling myself well enough in the interview.

Since then, I've had the opportunity to tell my story with confidence many times on different platforms only a year on from what I initially felt had been my biggest personal career disappointment.

Your story is really about recognising and communicating your worth and value which can often be found in the things you have overcome or experienced - after all, diamonds are made through the pressure they endure.

To be very clear - as a human being you already have inherent value, that doesn't need to be proven - whether it is because you believe like me that we're created in the image and likeness of God, or you believe in the value of human dignity without a connection to the divine.

I'm not saying if you don't have a story, you can't prove your worth, therefore you might have no worth. I'm saying we are all already intrinsically worthy and knowing and communicating our story reminds us of that. And it also reminds those we choose to work with and for what we practically bring to the table.

The simplest storytelling technique is about a hero, going through a challenge and coming to a resolution. This can include growing up as a single child, or in a family of 10, the languages you speak, a diagnosis, your unique place of struggle and resilience, where you have shown true creativity.

You are the hero of your story - so what are the unique challenges you have faced and how have you been able to resolve them? Your USP is buried in those answers.

A helping hand

This is where career coaching can be very useful. When working with me, we can look at leveraging your uniqueness, and creating a profile that emphasises the value you add.

Reflection: Your USP

1. What character traits make you unique?

2. What experiences have you had that are different to your current environment[6]?

3. What skills and achievements do you have that are different to your current environment?

The 'Honour in Weakness' perspective

Although the Soloist Impostor type is the one that most relishes not working with others, many of us do feel bad or inadequate or weird asking for help.

This is even though we can all rationalise that it is impossible for us to do everything ourselves.

Let's quickly look at how and why the other Impostor Types might struggle with asking for help:

- *Perfectionist:* has such a high standard, they find it hard to delegate

- *Expert:* so desires to know everything themselves, they find it hard to rely on another's knowledge

- *Natural Genius:* needs to be able to do all things with ease and speed, which blocks others from helping

- *Superwoman:* also, inherently a solo act

Yet, we honour others' strengths when we come to them with our weaknesses. Think about it - most of us don't expect to know all we can about health and healing and would be happy to speak to a doctor; most of us don't know everything about law, so we'll hire a lawyer; or about taxes, so we'll hire an accountant.

And if you are an entrepreneur or contractor, your clients are honouring your strength in the place of their weakness.

This is how the world goes round - it's the basis of the economy, trading what we don't have and want or need with what we do have.

But with many of us trying to DIY everything either out of curiosity or because we don't have the funds to hire the right people right now, we are slowly beginning to erode that honour for others' abilities for the sake of being part-time or freelance soloists.

However, some of the most successful people are successful because they outsource everything that isn't in their 'zone of genius' - the sweet spot between what you are great at and what energises and satisfies you[7].

Don't get me wrong - I have really enjoyed learning how to transform packs of Colour 1B[8] Expressions extensions into jumbo braids on my head during the pandemic. I'm proud of myself for making do when not being able to access a hairdresser due to COVID regulations. However, I can tell you now that blocking out 12-15 hours of my Saturday every 6 weeks to do my hair was not the one for me!

I've learned how to do my hair myself to a satisfactory standard, and although I love the outcome, I absolutely hate the process. I cannot wait to delegate this particular task back to someone faster and more talented than me as soon as possible!

Away from leisure DIY activities, especially as new entrepreneurs we can fall into the trap of being a jack of all trades, master of none, but we need to flee that temptation. Yes, we might not be able to afford hiring people's services immediately, but we could do skill swaps, or check out their free resources and ensure we are budgeting and planning our business goals to hire these people someday.

About 6 months into my self employed journey, I tried to DIY my whole social media strategy to the same level of other coaching and counselling businesses that had professional Marketing departments or personnel working on it.

Every day, I would sweat over colour hex codes, wording, tone of voice, hashtags, grid placement etc. while also creating daily content.

After 2 months of daily 'perfect' posting, a nice increase in followers and likes, but no sales whatsoever, I ended up close to burn out and feeling very resentful towards social media.

It got so bad, just thinking about posting something on Instagram made me feel anxious and overwhelmed. So, I responded the usual way I deal with overwhelm, by taking several steps back and withdrawing.

For 3 months I stopped posting completely, because I realised I hated having to think about content creation work. All I really wanted to do was support my clients as a coach and counsellor, but because I know how important awareness is to get to the place of even having clients, I poured my all into social media work.

The problem was that social media work is not my zone of genius. So not only did I end up resentful of it, I also spent most of my time doing tasks that I didn't feel competent at and that did the opposite of energising me, thereby making me feel more like an Impostor entrepreneur.

Also, using other people's strategies who have a different personality and different set of abilities to me, did not work. What I should have done and what I will be doing in future is hire the people with that experience and passion, or skill swap with those talented in my network who are happy to help me.

I've already had a very positive experience of working with others in our respective 'zones of genius' through this book. Initially, I was tempted to DIY my book cover - Canva makes stuff look easy, am I right sis?

Upon further reflection I knew it would take me more time and effort than I had to spare, considering that I was the only one who could actually write my book, so I had to prioritise time for that.

Therefore, hiring Sabrina as my graphic designer felt both like an act of self-care and a strategic business move.

Plus, no matter how much time I would have invested in Canva, my cover would have never looked as fire as it does now thanks to Sabrina.

So, while Sabrina was working on the cover, I would continue the writing, motivated by the ideas she would share with me.

Instead of feeling like an Impostor because I was working outside my zone of genius, I could marvel at Sabrina's genius, while expressing my own through writing my story.

Thinking of your own profession, for a moment, how offensive would it be if someone came to you and told you after a day, a week, or a month of self-learning, they are acceptably competent in achieving the same goals you do now, with your years of experience and education? Wouldn't that be offensive? Yet, we do the same thing trying to be all things and do all things for ourselves.

Reflection: Zone of Genius

1. Where do you consistently and verifiably get good results for others and yourself?

2. What work do you do that doesn't really feel like work?

3. What work do you do that you are most satisfied with?

The intersection of those answers is likely your zone of genius.

Key Ideas

- Reframing = all about different perspectives
- I introduced 3 perspectives to challenge Impostor thoughts:
    - ***The Humankind perspective:*** we all experience doubt
    - ***The Personal History perspective:*** your story is your USP
    - ***The 'Honour in Weakness' Perspective:*** honour others' strengths in your weaknesses, flow in your zone of genius

Endnotes

1 APA (2020)

2 Study.com (2020)

3 Sakulku & Alexander (2011)

4 Cruz (2009)

5 Hanks (2016)

6 Your current environment might make you feel like an Alien or like a Clone, but remember you can still leverage that

7 Wiest (2018)

8 Colour 1B: A popular colour name for hair extensions which matches many Black women's natural Black hair colour

CHAPTER 12

A: Adaptability

"All failure is failure to adapt,
all success is successful adaptation."

MAX MCKEOWN

The world is forever changing. Yet, change is something many people struggle with. Until I entered the working world, I didn't realise how many adults struggle with change.

I didn't realise, because I was unknowingly raised to be a change expert - I have two mother tongues, I've lived on 3 continents, across 4 countries, attended 7 different schools from primary to university education and am currently residing in my 8th city. It still blows my mind to this day.

Was there a time I hated change? Absolutely! Leaving friends and familiarity every time my family moved wasn't fun. But the older I got, the more I recognised I was being taught a very valuable life skill - adaptability.

“

I was unknowingly raised to be a change expert - I have two mother tongues, I've lived on 3 continents, across 4 countries, attended 7 different schools from primary to university education and am currently residing in my 8th city.

”

Adaptability is defined as *"the capacity to make appropriate responses to changed or changing situations; the ability to modify or adjust one's behaviour in meeting different circumstances or different people"*[1]. Learning to be adaptable is the same as learning to manage change well[2].

What does this have to do with Impostor Syndrome I hear you ask? Well, it can be argued that there is an overlap between anxiety caused by change and anxiety caused by feeling like a fraud, especially as Impostor Syndrome is often triggered by a change in circumstances, ambitions, level of responsibility etc.

Therefore, to reduce feelings of Impostor Syndrome, it is helpful to reduce the co-anxiety effect of Impostor Syndrome and change, by learning to be more adaptable in the face of change.

As mentioned before, managing change well has been my bread and butter for years, and my appointment to my first paid manager role brought my adaptability skills into the professional realm.

My appointment, as previously discussed, immediately unleashed an almighty dose of Impostor Syndrome in me. This was especially because it was a double promotion (2 jumps up the pay and responsibility scale) and the role had been unmanaged for 5 months with project deadlines looming.

Add to that, at the time, I was the youngest manager and only Black person in the 60+ person department, I didn't have project management qualifications (a fact my Expert Impostor Type didn't let me forget), and I also have a 'minority specific' chronic illness (Sickle Cell Anaemia[3]).

The confidence I had during the interview stage evaporated before the job even officially started.

I learned the hard way what "learning on the job" means and although I wish my season of adapting to the new wouldn't have been as brutal as it was on my mental and physical health, I did come out of it with a set of mature problem solving and change management skills that gave my struggle some purpose.

So much so that when I was asked to move to a different management role a year and some later to help cover business needs, I embraced it as a chance to test my skills, rather than moan about the fact I was only just getting used to my new normal.

What exactly helped me become more adaptable I hear you ask?

Growing resilience and creating structure.

Growing resilience

In my time as a manager resilience was a core competency for me to embrace for myself and to model to my team. The model of resilience that stuck out to me most and one I even gave a department wide training on, is the i-resilience model by Robertson-Cooper[4]. This model relies on 4 key components that facilitate resilience:

1. Confidence
2. Social Support
3. Adaptability and
4. Purposefulness

Figure 4: The 4 components of the i-resilience model (RobertsonCooper, 2021)

Increasing resilience then requires us to invest in growing these 4 components.

Confidence:

- feeling competent and effective in coping with stressful situations
- having strong self esteem
- able to regulate emotions

This is why dealing with Impostor Syndrome boosts our confidence as it tackles all of the above.

Social Support:

- having good relationships with others
- successfully being able to seek support when in need

We've touched on some of this already and will expand further on this in the Defence part of The F.R.A.U.D. Framework™.

Adaptability:

- flexibility in the face of situations beyond our control
- accepting and recovering from change faster

My framework can help with this, and so can training on change management or therapy in grief and loss.

Purposefulness:

- having a clear sense of purpose, values, drive
- a clear sense of direction

This is where life planning or life coaching can help.

Reflection: Resilience Monitor

1. Which element of resilience do you feel you struggle with the least right now?

2. Which element of resilience do you feel you struggle with the most right now?

3. How could you practically increase your resilience based on the 4 areas?

Creating structure

While growing my level of resilience helped me mentally, it was recognising and fully understanding patterns in the way things were done in my environment and then developing a framework around them that helped me practically.

Capturing standard operating procedures saved my team and I time and hassle. In fact, recruiting a team was the first and most impactful structure for me. You see, it wasn't until I had 3 other people working full-time hours beside me based on the job descriptions I had created and responsibilities I had delegated to them that I realised, the problem wasn't that I was a fraud; the problem was that I was trying to do 4 people's full-time jobs!

Had I not taken the time to outline exactly what tasks needed doing in my new role, measured how long they took and brought those insights to my manager, who then realised I needed more help, I would have kept feeling inadequate.

Another one of these structures I created was my own onboarding framework, the *7 Ts of Onboarding*™ which didn't just help me onboard myself into my job, but through my workshops has also helped many others learn to manage change better, whether in their personal or professional lives.

In fact, in most of my workshops, I have been using dealing with the COVID-19 pandemic as an example of how to practically apply the *7 Ts of Onboarding*™ to your everyday life.

Reflection: Mapping Processes

1. Do you know the average length all the tasks you do at your workplace take? If not, why not take some time to test it out?

2. Once you know the average length of your tasks, do you have enough hours in your working week to do them justice?

Specific Application - The Perfectionist

The Perfectionist might benefit most from intentionally creating structures. This is because we already know that taking the time to create 'perfect' templates once, might save The Perfectionist time and stress for many other contexts.

Similarly, creating structures or frameworks to help them manage change may also reduce their time fretting over not knowing how to cope with the change perfectly.

A helping hand

I'll be releasing a short book on the 7 *Ts of Onboarding*™ at some point, but if you want to work through the framework sooner, feel free to sign up to one of my Boss Your Impostor Type Coaching Programmes here: https://blueprintway.com/byit-wl

Minding Margins

There is one more, very important lesson I learned about becoming more adaptable *after* I had left my management role and was recovering from mental and emotional burnout - the need to mind my margins.

In business, profit margins refer to what's left from your income after the cost of production has been deducted from the sale price.

In the world of Emotional Wealth, which is the core focus of my business The Blueprint Way™, margins refer to the breathing spaces we leave for eventualities, AFTER already making space for rest. They are like the mental health equivalent of an emergency fund.

The premise of minding your margins is based on the truth that we can't always predict change, but we can better prepare for it by leaving space for it.

During the increasingly strategically chaotic and emotionally distressing restructure process, I had been so busy and high strung trying to be the best manager I knew to be to my team and senior stakeholders, it wasn't a surprise I ended up crashing and burning out - sidelined by my chronic illness, because I had ignored my mental health for too long.

On top of my demanding job, at the time, I was also:

- studying to be a counsellor at a centre 1 hour drive each way from where I lived;
- doing my counselling placement with up to 4 clients a week *after* work;
- completing course assignments weekly and
- being a newlywed wife.

Every moment of my life was meticulously planned out and my only true 'free time' was when I was sleeping.

Whenever we choose to put ourselves under overwhelming pressure, it distracts us from being in a position of strategic planning as well as hinders resource preservation and accumulation.

So, if any unforeseen change or an emergency happens there is nothing left to address that, because all our resources are wrapped up in maintaining our status quo. The change or emergency then likely becomes more critical and disruptive than it could have been, had we left some margins.

In my case, I wasn't going to change my marital status, or even stop my studies to cope with the pressure at work better. However, I could have looked at how to relieve the pressure at work in the first place, even if it meant setting firmer boundaries with overtime work for example.

I needed to focus on doing whatever was necessary to maintain my physical and mental health emergency funds, instead of recklessly depleting them.

I was too busy trying to be The Superwoman, instead of delegating and prioritising where I could.

Does this sound familiar to you? It might well be a different context but the reality of not having margins in your life might be depleting all your resources too.

Reflection: Margin Maintenance

1. Do you have margins in your life?

2. Where do you need margins in your life?

3. What small step can you take towards establishing margins in your life?

Specific Application - The Superwoman

The Superwoman is usually least mindful of her margins and needs to make an extra effort to put free time on her schedule. Please beware - if you continue at that pace, a burnout won't be far off.

The same way a financial emergency fund can help us weather unforeseen storms, a mental health emergency fund can too. But you need to invest into it now for there to be something to draw on later. The Defence part of The F.R.A.U.D. Framework™ will explore how to do so in more detail.

A helping hand

If you are overwhelmed by change happening to you in life or work at the moment, or if you are hoping to implement lasting change, contact me to explore working with me as a coach.

Key Ideas

- There is a co-anxiety effect between change and Impostor Syndrome
- Adaptability = appropriately respond to changed or changing situations
- 3 frameworks to increase Adaptability were introduced:
- i-resilience Model by Robertson-Cooper
- 7Ts of Onboarding™ by Vanetta Morrison
- Emotional Wealth: Mind your margins

Endnotes

1 VandenBos (2015)

2 Zhou & Lin (2016)

3 Sickle Cell Anaemia: a hereditary, multi system chronic blood disorder most commonly diagnosed in people of African, Caribbean, Indian, Mediterranean and Middle Eastern descent

4 RobertsonCooper (2021)

CHAPTER 13

U: Understanding

"Knowledge breeds confidence. Confidence destroys fear. Destroy your fear"

ROBERT KIYOSAKI

The **Understanding** element in The F.R.A.U.D. Framework™ is about expressing and cultivating your expertise on your subject matter of choice. This is done by examining both how well you can explain your subject to others and how aware you are of current trends in the field.

Increasing understanding can stop you from feeling like you might be an A grade student, who is only good at passing the necessary exams, but an F grade practitioner, who is terrible at doing it in real life.

Share what you know

Many of us know that one of the best ways to prove your understanding of something is to teach it to someone else. This might not be in a classic classroom context, but you can write books or articles, record videos, give talks etc. on the subject matter to teach others and simultaneously to remind yourself of how well you know it.

A further benefit of creating content to communicate and teach to others, is that it develops your portfolio of resources and can inspire you to research and innovate further, thereby turning you into the expert you don't think you are.

“

Experts become experts by engaging with a subject matter in depth through study and continual application and innovation. If you are teaching others about, constantly growing and engaging with, and creating new developments in your area of expertise, then you are not an Impostor.

”

Grow what you know

Understanding is also the step where you consider how much you are participating in continual professional development in your area and, where necessary, commit to more.

You might want to take additional courses, read up on the latest developments or attend relevant conferences to ensure your subject knowledge is evidence based and up to date.

Experts become experts by engaging with a subject matter in depth through study and continual application and innovation. If you are teaching others about, constantly growing and engaging with, and creating new developments in your area of expertise, then you are not an Impostor.

Reflection: Knowledge Base

1. What topics can you confidently teach (speak, write, record, run a session) on?

2. What topics do you want to be taught at a professional level?

Specific Application - The Expert

The Expert Impostor Type in particular struggles with mostly considering their level of knowledge and understanding as inadequate. Yet, it is important to recognise that your inherent human value is not determined by your level of knowledge or lack thereof. Instead, being clear on the topics you have advanced knowledge on and going deeper into those, frees you from the unrealistic burden of having to be omniscient.

Remember, the areas you don't have expertise in can be where you can find honour in your weakness by honouring others' expertise.

As a confessing Expert myself, this step of The F.R.A.U.D. Framework™ continues to be the most important one in helping me boss my own Impostor Syndrome. In fact, this very book you are reading is a manifestation of me seeking to widen my understanding of Impostor Syndrome and then teach it to others.

Also, each time I'm working with a client and explaining some psychological term or giving short psychoeducation in sessions, as I share my understanding of these topics, I learn to trust my understanding and expertise of these topics more.

A helping hand

If you are interested in working with me on positioning yourself as an expert in your field, contact me to discuss a personalised coaching experience.

Key Ideas

- Express and cultivate expertise in your subject matter
- Experts become experts through deep study and continual application of their subject area
- Lack of knowledge is not failure, but a signal for a growth area

CHAPTER 14

D: Defence

"Good riddance to decisions that don't support self-care, self-value and self-worth."

OPRAH WINFREY

As mentioned in the introduction of this book, there is no one time cure for Impostor Syndrome. I can't get you to stop doubting yourself forever or stop your environment from making you doubt yourself, but hopefully I can help you to reduce the times you do and inspire you to choose courage and confidence instead.

Defence is about using positive input to proactively defend yourself against the negative and false thoughts and feelings of being an Impostor. This can be done by:

- adhering to a healthy self-care routine
- remembering and embracing positive self-talk as well as
- cultivating a community of others who affirm you in your skills, abilities, and experience

“

As with money in a bank account the body budget requires continual investment into it, so as not to bankrupt it.

”

Self-Care Routine

It is better to be equipped and prepared to tackle Impostor Syndrome before it even begins. Self-care is all about ensuring you are looking after your health and wellbeing in a proactive and holistic way.

During my research on what contributes to a good life, I came across a concept called 'body budget' which states the essentials of physical health are good sleep, a healthy diet and regular exercise[1]. As with money in a bank account the body budget requires continual investment into it, so as not to bankrupt it.

Many of us have heard of the importance of good sleep to our health, yet many adults across the world are sleep-deprived [2]. Think about the last time you had 7-9 hours sleep per night, the recommended number of hours for adults?

Add to that reported surges of insomnia due to the COVID-19 pandemic[3], and it's clear most of us are doing the best we can, without the basics of good sleep to help us regulate our mood and weight, lower our risk of illness, think more clearly, and make good decisions[4].

I mention sleep here as it seems the easiest one of the three to tackle - but there are reams and reams of books written and speeches spoken about the impact of a healthy diet and exercise on our overall health. Suffice it to say, our physical health can pose a great risk to our mental health and sometimes battling our Impostor Syndrome starts with making ourselves a healthy meal and going to bed at a decent time.

Other self-care spheres include keeping on top of our medical appointments (#CallYourDentist #BookYourSmearTest), taking time for hobbies and interests, and maintaining a clean and tidy home which acts as a safe space for us.

There are many more examples of self-care that might be more specific to you, so it is important to take the time to identify what routines work best for you.

An easy way to check your self-care reserves is by doing the *'HALT' test* - are you **h**ungry, **a**ngry/anxious/annoyed, **l**onely/low, or **t**ired? If yes, it's high time to halt your decision making and instead attend to some self-care before you end up making permanent decisions based on temporary feelings.

Once upon a time, someone sold us the lie that self-care is selfish and since then many of us have been bending over backwards for others at the cost of our impending burnout and resentment (I'm especially talking to all my Superwoman Impostors/model minorities out there).

But even if we have come around to the idea that we can't pour out of an empty cup and therefore self-care actually helps us to sustainably serve others better, by default, most of our minds and lives are set up to deny ourselves at a moment's notice, for the sake of others. Therefore, to practice self-care routines consistently, healthy boundaries are required.

I define healthy boundaries as *"interpersonal rules of engagement that set the context of all my interactions with others, based on having taken my purpose, worth and needs into consideration first".*

Being raised as a Christian model minority I learned early to 'think of myself less' as C.S. Lewis' definition of humility goes[5].

However, it didn't take long for me to confuse that with 'thinking less of myself' and suddenly everyone else's needs but mine seemed to be considered.

I spent years trapped in the deception of confusing inferiority with humility, and it took a re-education in my faith as well as challenging my cultural background to recognise being humble and having boundaries are not mutually exclusive.

So, when I say I take my purpose, worth and needs into consideration first, it is not coming from a place of arrogance or pride. Instead, it is coming from the realisation that I have a unique purpose in my life (as do we all) and my most important task is to align with that purpose and serve people from that place of purpose with excellence.

Of course, if there is a genuine emergency and someone needs my help, I won't deny it. Our boundaries aren't there to excuse us from helping others in need.

But setting boundaries does challenge what we deem as an emergency. Just because someone has flagged their situation as urgent, doesn't mean it really is urgent.

Going back to the point of Impostor Syndrome being proactively fought against with good sleep for example, my phone automatically goes on 'Do not disturb' (DND) at a certain time every night. Which means I don't receive any calls or messages from anyone, except my closest family members, so they can contact me in case of an emergency.

Otherwise, everything else can wait until the morning, AFTER a good night's sleep.

If I didn't turn my phone on DND, I would at times be kept awake by WhatsApp messages from family and friends in different time zones to me, about nothing urgent - many times even nothing important, until the early hours of the morning.

I also had to teach myself to not pick up the phone to everyone, anytime it rings. Gyles still marvels at the fact that I can ignore spontaneous calls from family and friends, no matter who it is. He didn't know me in the years when I was literally living my life at the beck and call of others and only doing what I needed to do for myself in between, if at all.

Thankfully, training to become a counsellor taught me how to set boundaries that ultimately benefit my loved ones, my clients and me. It's the 'oxygen mask on a plane principle' at play - boundaries are the markers you set, that protect you from rushing to fix someone else's oxygen mask, when yours isn't on yet.

Your boundaries can prevent a number of issues, such as ill health, burnout, or resentment.

Reflection: Self-care & Boundaries

1. Are you practising enough self-care?

2. How much sleep do you get on average each night?

3. Have you set healthy boundaries for yourself?

Specific Application - The Superwoman

Of course, maintaining a healthy self-care routine is necessary for all Impostor Types, but The Superwoman might be most likely to have completely abandoned hers. As The Superwoman lives for the fulfilment of the needs of others to affirm her sense of worth, she often ends up burnt out, resentful or bitter.

I can say from both my personal and professional life observations of Black women in particular, that we need to be reminded that rest is our birthright, regardless of whether we feel like we earned it or not.

Positive Affirmations

Positive self-affirmations are declarations of encouragement designed to strengthen our sense of self when *habitually spoken* and *intentionally lived.* Let's dive a little deeper into this definition.

1. Habitually Spoken

Many of us may have already heard about positive affirmations and some of us may have even already tried them, to no avail. Yet, there is scientific research[6] providing an evidence base that positive affirmations, also referred to as positive self-talk, make a measurable difference to both the quality and longevity of people's lives. To access those benefits, consistency is key.

This is because our brain naturally reinforces what is already common to us (known as Confirmation Bias[7]), so if we commonly think negatively, our brain is more inclined to think negatively and even predict future outcomes to be more negative.

But if we consistently train our brain to think positively, it will gradually change its default expectation mechanism to challenge our negative defaults and maybe even expect more positive outcomes.

2. Intentionally Lived

But some research[8] shows, affirmations don't just work because we say so. We can't just speak ourselves healthier for example. In fact, for people with low self-esteem, if their affirmations are the complete opposite of their current lives, positive affirmations can end up being detrimental to their mental health.

For affirmations to work for us, they need to be aligned with our existing values[9]. If we don't value success or don't consider ourselves as successful for example, repeating 'I embody success' to yourself will be more ruinous than reassuring.

That's because the blatant incongruence between what you are saying and what you truly believe will increase feelings of self-doubt and being a fraud.

To reduce this incongruence and feelings of fraudulence, we can choose to:

- work on our core beliefs and/or
- work on our values and/or
- focus on affirmations already aligned with our values (the easiest option) so that we can end up intentionally living towards the realisation of the affirmations.

When doing so, it is not about being perfect in accomplishing the truth of the affirmation. Instead, research shows that committing our best effort towards the fulfilment of the affirmation is more helpful than aiming for a specific level of competence.

The Power of Affirmations

There is ample research out there that heralds the benefits of talking to ourselves with more compassion and optimism[10]. Among many other things, positive affirmations are said to:

- Reduce stress
- Improve quality of life
- Reduce pain
- Increase life expectancy and
- Boost the immune system[11].

It's like the multivitamins of psychology - a great supplement to an already nutritious diet.

But remember, supplements can only help so much if our staple diet is unhealthy - it's the same way with affirmations.

They can only help so much if our overall mental health is deteriorating. Should you be in a mental health crisis, affirmations aren't your best bet, speaking to a specialist is.

Reflection: Positive Self-Talk

1. Is your self-talk predominantly positive or negative?

2. What affirmation can you believe that is aligned with your values?

Social Support and Feedback from others

Impostor Syndrome thrives when we feel isolated, so having people in your corner who can give you love, and care is always a good defence against feeling like you don't belong.

Add to that having people in your corner who also truly recognise the value you bring in your field and it is a great defence against unwanted and untrue thoughts and feelings about your worth and abilities.

You shouldn't feel like you need to force it to feel accepted, so instead of working to find your tribe among those who are consciously or unconsciously rejecting you, start or invest in your own tribe.

Your tribe are those people who get you, get where you are going, support you, are not jealous or intimidated by your growth but are committed to and celebrate it as their own AND will tell you about yourself when you need it.

They are not fair-weather friends. Your tribe also includes your loyal and engaging clients/ customers who can provide you constructive feedback.

Personally, I have often been able to downplay my skills or the achievement of my qualifications.

But I struggle with downplaying client after client telling me I have helped change their lives through counselling or coaching or showing me increased customer satisfaction rates and recruitment targets because of my project or change management.

I either start believing they are all liars or just trying to make me feel good, or I start accepting that my perceptions of myself are not always right. I may have to accept that I do know what I'm doing and that my successes are not down to luck, but hard work and talent.

One of my business coaches talks about keeping a 'brag bank' - a place where you store all your positive feedback from clients, customers, and colleagues - this can then also double up as positive self-talk as you remind yourself of the value you provide through the eyes of your customers.

From my experience, having my own mentors, coaches, and counsellors to reach out to on a regular basis, also helps me to proactively reduce the amount of Impostor moments I experience.

This is because I am accountable to them for any growth I have committed to; challenged by them if I'm going off-track; and reassured by them that I'm on the right path and that I'm already adding value now, not just hoping to do so in a distant future.

Reflection: Social Support

1. Have you got a tribe?

2. Who is part of your psychological safe space?

3. Who could you make part of your psychological safe space?

Specific Application - The Soloist, The Alien and The Abused

The Soloist Impostor Type might struggle most with this step of cultivating and relying on a social support system. But every Type can and should benefit from a community of constructive cheerleaders providing encouragement, feedback, and support to you when needed.

Having such a community is also particularly important for The Alien and The Abused. The Alien needs people around them who make them feel less like an alien and more like they truly belong. The Abused needs people around them who reinforce the psychological safety they had been deprived of due to the abuse.

A helping hand

If you tend to only see the negative or inadequate aspects of yourself, it is especially important to get external feedback from others or even get some counselling. You can contact me to find out more about my counselling services.

Key Ideas

- Not possible to completely eradicate Impostor Syndrome, but possible to reduce it, through practical tools to grow your capacity and margins
- Actively defending yourself from Impostor attacks through:
- Healthy self-care routines
- Positive affirmations
- Good social support

Endnotes

1 Lukanovich (2020)

2 Statista (2016)

3 Lufkin (2021)

4 Health.gov (2021)

5 His quote: 'Humility is not thinking less of yourself, it's thinking of yourself less.'

6 Positive Psychology (2021)

7 APA Dictionary of Psychology (2021)

8 Wood et al. (2009)

9 Rose . n.d.

10 Positive Psychology (2021)

11 Healthline.com (2020)

Summary

We've delved deep into the world of Impostor Syndrome, so here is a summary of all the key points we covered:

Impostor Syndrome (IS) is defined as a persistent experience of inadequacy, incompetence and context-specific isolation in which objective successes are discounted or attributed to anything other than personal effort and ability.

We identified that both nature (personality) and nurture (socialisation) can increase the prevalence of Impostor feelings.

IS is a cross-cultural, cross-generational, cross-class and cross-gender issue. However, women of colour living at the intersection of racism, sexism and misogyny (aka misogynoir) are particularly prone to IS.

Societal pressure exists that women can *have* it all, only if they can *do* and *be* it all too.

Though not a classified mental illness, there is a high correlation of IS with mental illnesses like depression & anxiety.

Valerie Young identified 5 Impostor subtypes:

- *The Perfectionist:* feels like a fraud if they can't do things perfectly

- *The Expert:* feels like a fraud if they lack knowledge/qualifications in an area

- *The Natural Genius:* feels like a fraud if they don't succeed with ease on the 1st try
- *The Superwoman:* feels like a fraud if they can't juggle all their responsibilities flawlessly
- *The Soloist:* feels like a fraud if they can't achieve success on their own

I proposed we can reframe Young's Impostor Types for our benefit, by recognising their strengths and mitigating for their weaknesses.

A set of action steps were proposed to start the reframing process:

- From Perfectionist to Quality Assurance Specialist
- From Expert to Student Teacher
- From Natural Genius to Person of Influence
- From Superwoman to Queen of Boundaries
- From Soloist to Interdependent Adult

Many challenges we face could be down to underlying fears of inadequacy, incompetence and isolation.

Our Impostor subtype may influence a multitude of our behaviours including how we procrastinate.

I proposed 4 Procrastinator Types and how they related to the Impostor Types, as well as action steps to stop procrastinating with each type:

- *The Hater:* the task at hand it not enjoyable at all - relatable to all Impostor Types

- *The Overwhelmed:* the task at hand is too much to manage - especially resonates with The Superwoman and The Soloist

- *The Thinker:* fear of the task leads to analysis paralysis in starting it - especially resonates with The Perfectionist and The Expert

- *The Non-Committer:* the task is not as exciting as the next cool idea - especially resonates with The Natural Genius

Impostor Exotypes focus on how our environment can affect how we see ourselves as Impostors. I introduced 4 Impostor Exotypes that further explain this influence:

- *The Alien:* we are made to feel like the odd one out

- *The Clone:* we are made to feel like the outdated model

- *The Abused:* we are made to feel worthless

- *The Codependent:* we are made to feel incapable of caring for ourselves

These Impostor Exotypes can be reframed for our benefit too. However, it's important to create psychological safe spaces before engaging in the work of challenging the Impostor role society is pushing on you, to avoid feeling completely isolated or alone.

If we choose to accept the reframed purposes of the Exotypes, they provide steps towards the transformation of:

- Alien to Ambassador;
- Clone to Architect;
- Abused to Activist;
- Codependent to Agent of Self Actualisation

The F.R.A.U.D. Framework™ is designed to be your personal CBT tool to boss your Impostor Syndrome, based on the premise that to stop feeling like an Impostor, we need to stop thinking like one.

As we recognise that our feelings are not facts, rather they are clues to our thoughts, putting our thoughts on trial and deciding what is **Fact or Fiction** is necessary to change our Impostor thinking and eventually change our Impostor feelings.

Another way to change your thinking is through the process of **reframing**, or seeing things from a different perspective to our default.

I introduced 3 perspectives to challenge Impostor thoughts:

- *The Humankind perspective:* we all experience doubt
- *The Personal History perspective:* your story is your USP
- *The 'Honour in Weakness' Perspective:* honour others' strengths in your weaknesses, flow in your zone of genius

Because we can often feel anxious about change and Impostor Syndrome is usually triggered by some sort of change, it is important to develop our adaptability to change, to reduce the co-anxiety effect between change and Impostor Syndrome.

Adaptability refers to the ability to appropriately respond to changed or changing situations. To increase adaptability, 3 frameworks were introduced:

- i-resilience Model by Robertson-Cooper
- 7Ts of Onboarding™ by Vanetta Morrison
- Emotional Wealth: Mind your margins

Bossing our Impostor Syndrome is also done well by showing our **understanding** through expressing and cultivating expertise in our subject matter. Teaching others and committing to learning are important factors of bossing our Impostor Syndrome.

Experts become experts through deep study and continual application of their subject area and lack of knowledge is not failure, but a signal for a potential growth area.

Finally, we learned that it isn't possible to completely eradicate Impostor Syndrome, but it is possible to reduce its intensity and disruption to our lives, through practical tools to grow our capacity and margins, that act as a **defence.**

We can actively defend ourselves from Impostor attacks through:

- Healthy self-care routines
- Positive affirmations
- Good social support

Limitations

Although I have covered a lot in this book, there is so much more to say about Impostor Syndrome.

I acknowledge my limitations specifically in exploring how Impostor Syndrome affects queer women of colour or disabled women of colour. The more intersections of oppression we face, the more Impostor Syndrome can hinder our lives.

I'm also mindful of the fact that The F.R.A.U.D. Framework™ does not sufficiently address the external pressures, discrimination and oppression we face that can make us feel like Impostors.

Because of the magnitude of these oppressions, writers and researchers on diversity and inclusion topics like Ruchika Tulshyan, Jodi-Ann Burey and Ebony McGee are petitioning to stop misdiagnosing women with Impostor Syndrome.

Instead, they are advocating to call out and fight the structural racism at play that makes us feel like we don't belong in the first place.

I completely agree that structural racism and sexism are primarily to blame for creating an environment in which many women of colour, and especially Black women are made to feel inadequate, incompetent and isolated.

If we are implicitly or explicitly told that success never looks like us or should never look like us, then of course it will be hard for us to internalise our own.

Yet, even with external forces creating the conditions for Impostor Syndrome to flourish, we can still end up inheriting the false and racist narrative that seeks to hold us back.

These internal blockers are what I want to help us confront, even as the work to dismantle the structural blockers desperately needs doing too.

I hope exploring and discussing all the research in the book has made it clear, my desire is not to point the finger at us and tell us to do better. We are already doing exceptionally well given the crap we are often exposed to.

Instead, my desire is to educate us to recognise both what is going on internally and externally whenever we feel like we are a fraud and like we don't belong. My desire is also to equip us to challenge the part of ourselves that continues to foster Impostor thoughts.

I'm pointing the finger at Impostor Syndrome, in the hope that we will no longer let it get away with bossing us about.

Having researched and seen different ways of tackling Impostor Syndrome, I'm also mindful of the fact that my approach is more thought and behaviour change based, than physical.

Yet, with Impostor Syndrome being experienced by some as a type of trauma, only focusing on thoughts can do them a disservice. There is a growing body of research on the benefits of somatic experiencing on trauma work and some of those insights may prove useful to tackling Impostor Syndrome too.

Especially as we spoke about the need for psychological safe spaces to help us do the work of bossing Impostor Syndrome, we need to understand how our body reacts to a space is core to whether we mentally judge it as safe or not.

For a more body-centred approach to tackling Impostor Syndrome, check out the workshop by Health Coach Natisha Willis: **http://www.natishawillis.com/freein4 .**

Conclusion

Feeling like an Impostor from time to time is a normal part of the human experience. The important thing to remember is to not let a moment of Impostor Syndrome pick up momentum and become a mindset.

It is normal for these moments to also repeat themselves in the future, but they don't have to be crippling. So, the next time Impostor Syndrome rears its ugly head, remember you have F.R.A.U.D. as a tool to boss the beast!

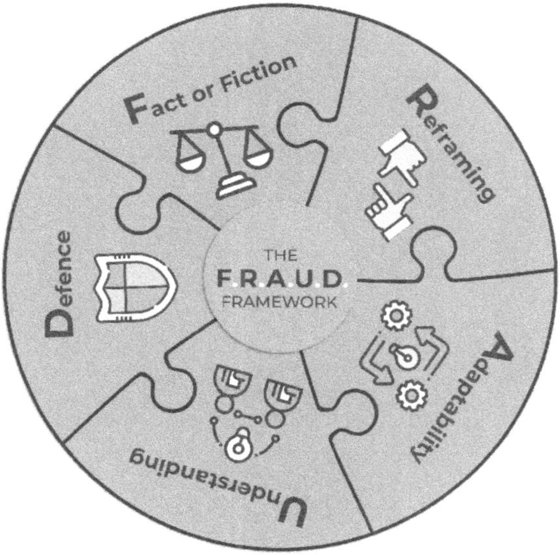

What's next?

Thanks again for purchasing and reading this book. I appreciate Impostor Syndrome is something you want help to boss, and I hope this book has helped you.

If you'd like to join my Boss Your Impostor Type Coaching Programme to work through tools and exercises in a safe space with a community of like-minded women of colour, sign up on:
https://blueprintway.com/byit-wl/

If you need any further help exploring issues of anxiety, self-worth, negative thoughts, or career progression and life planning, feel free to contact me so we can discuss which of my coaching or counselling services might be best suited to you.

To let me know how you get on with bossing your Impostor Syndrome or to seek further help from me, feel free to email me at:
vanetta@blueprintway.com

Acknowledgements

The saying goes that it takes a village to raise a child, and although writing a book is not the same as carrying and then raising a child, I would like to acknowledge the village of people who have supported me in getting this book from conception to delivery:

My husband, Gyles Morrison - who was both my loudest cheerleader and my most honest critic.

My graphic designer, Sabrina Brown - without the strong vision your designs created this project would have perished many times.

My editor, Letitia Jeffers - thank you for keeping it real with me and for lending your expertise as a therapist and your lived experience as a Black woman to bring more of my soul into this work.

My proofreader, Olivia Pitt - thank you for allowing me to see the book come alive through your eyes. Your feedback was incredible.

My accountability sister, Tracy Amofa-Diatuo - thanks for kicking my butt when it needed to be kicked and for making me set realistic deadlines, lol.

Thank you to every family member and friend whose eyes lit up when I mentioned I was writing a book and who couldn't wait to be able to recommend it. Your faith in me got me through the hardest parts.

And last, but certainly not least, thank You Lord for giving me your passion to serve people, the ability to write, and a loving and supportive community to give me just the right amount of celebration and critique to get the best out of me.

Glossary

Ambivert: someone who can equally draw energy from both solitary and/or social activities.

Bae (Before anyone else): affectionate term often used to describe one's significant other

Cognitive Distortions: habitual thinking patterns that are mostly negative and inaccurate

Colour 1B: A popular colour name for hair extensions which matches many Black women's natural Black hair colour

Extravert: someone who draws energy most from social activities

Executive Board Member: a key decision maker in a business, member of the board of directors

The F.R.A.U.D. Framework™: a 5 step guide to boss Impostor Syndrome developed by Vanetta Morrison

Helicopter Parenting: hovering over every single detail of your child's life for the sake of protecting from all harm and promoting them towards success

Impostor Phenomenon: internal experience of intellectual phoniness

Impostor Subtypes: 5 distinct profiles reflecting the different ways symptoms of IS show up, identified by Dr. Valerie Young

Impostor Syndrome: "a persistent experience of inadequacy, incompetence and context-specific isolation in which objective successes are discounted or attributed to anything other than personal effort and ability.

Impostor Exotypes: 4 distinct profiles reflecting the different ways our external environment can trigger symptoms of IS to show up, identified by Vanetta Morrison

Introvert: someone who draws energy most from quiet or solitary activities

Margin (Emotional Wealth): breathing spaces we leave for eventualities, after already making space for rest. They are like the mental health equivalent of an emergency fund.

Mental Illness: health condition involving changes in emotion, thinking or behaviour, associated with distress and/or problems functioning in social, work or family activities.

Micromanage: desire to control every detail of an activity leading to exact instructions for the person executing them and scrutinising whether the instructions are followed

Minority Status Stress: different types of stresses ethnic minority groups are exposed to due to their minority status, such as racism and discrimination

Misogynoir: the distrust, hatred of, and violence towards Black women as seen in pop culture and proliferated in the historical and current daily experiences of Black women

Model Minority: stereotypical view of a minority group as being more successful than other minority groups with the former being viewed as the ideal example of a minority.

Pluralistic Ignorance: the false assumption that the majority believes or values something that they actually do not

Procrastination: Procrastination is the act of consistently and unnecessarily delaying or postponing what we believe we should be doing now

Reframing: the ability to see a situation from a different perspective to our default one, to uncover a possible variety of different interpretations

Restructure: a process taken by a business that involves the significant modification of a department's previous ways of operating in order to make it more efficient

Senior Responsible Owner: owner of the project's business case; primarily owns any risks of the project and responsible for ensuring the project meets its objectives

Sickle Cell Anaemia: a hereditary, multi system chronic blood disorder most commonly diagnosed in people of African, Caribbean, Indian, Mediterranean and Middle Eastern descent

S.MA.R.T. Goal: a goal that is specific, **m**easurable, **a**chievable, **r**elevant and **t**imely

Socialisation: a process of being taught the cultural and social norms of the community one grows up in

Therapeutic Alliance: cooperative working relationship with a trained professional built on empathy, acceptance and confidentiality.

Unique Selling Point: a distinguishing aspect of a product or service that makes it more appealing than its peers

Zone of Genius: the area in which your passions and strengths overlap leading you to provide consistently great results for yourself and others

Reference List

Abrams, A. (2018) 'Yes, Impostor Syndrome Is Real. Here's How to Deal With It.' *Time.* [Online] 20th June. Available from: https://time.com/5312483/how-to-deal-with-impostor-syndrome/ [Accessed 25/05/20].

APA (American Psychological Association) (2020) *Reframing.* [Online]. Available from: https://dictionary.apa.org/reframing [Accessed 25/10/21].

APA Dictionary of Psychology (2021) *Confirmation Bias.* [Online]. Available from: https://dictionary.apa.org/confirmation-bias [Accessed 15/09/21].

Bailey, M. and Trudy (2018) On misogynoir: citation, erasure, and plagiarism, *Feminist Media Studies,* 18 (4), pp. 762-768.

Biddlecombe, S. n.d. 'Michelle Obama's words will resonate with anyone who lives with imposter syndrome', *Stylist,* [Online] n.d. Available from: https://www.stylist.co.uk/long-reads/michelle-obama-impostor-syndrome-career-advice-work-mental-health-relationships-becoming-book-us/240417 [Accessed 15/10/21].

Bravata, D. M., Madhusudhan D. K. Boroff, M., and Cokley, K. O. (2020) Commentary: Prevalence, Predictors, and Treatment of Imposter Syndrome: A Systematic Review. *Journal of Mental Health & Clinical Psychology,* 4 (3), pp. 12-16.

Cambridge Dictionary (2021) *Sexism.* [Online]. Available from: https://dictionary.cambridge.org/dictionary/english/sexism [Accessed 06/10/21].

Clance, P. R. (1985a) *The Impostor Phenomenon: Overcoming the fear that haunts your success.* Georgia: Peachtree Publishers.

Clance, P.R. (1985b) *The impostor phenomenon: When success makes you feel like a fake*. New York: Bantam Books.

Clance, P. R., Dingman, D., Reviere, S. L., & Stober, D. R. (1995) Impostor phenomenon in an interpersonal/social context: Origins and treatment. *Women & Therapy*, 16, pp. 79–96.

Clance, P. R. and Imes, S. (1978) The Imposter Phenomenon in High Achieving Women: Dynamics and Therapeutic Intervention, *Psychotherapy Theory, Research and Practice,* 15 (3), pp. 1-8.

Clance, P. R., & O'Toole, M. A. (1988) The impostor phenomenon: An internal barrier to empowerment and achievement. *Women and Therapy*, 6 (3), pp. 51-64.

Cokley, K., McClain, S., Enciso, A., & Martinez, M. (2013) An examination of the impact of minority status stress and impostor feelings on the mental health of diverse ethnic minority college students. *Journal of Multicultural Counseling and Development*, 41, pp. 82–95.

Cruz, P. (2009) *An Visit with Penelope Cruz* [Interview], The Envelope Please with J Blackstone, 1 February 2009.

Cusak, C. E., Hughes, J. L., and Nuhu, N. (2013) Connecting Gender and Mental Health to Impostor Phenomenon Feelings, *Journal of Psychological Research*, 18 (2), pp. 74-81.

Dictionary.com 2021, *Misogyny,* Retrieved: 6 October 2021, from: https://www.dictionary.com/browse/misogyny

Donahue, K., Gilbert, T., Halpert, M., and Robertson Migas, P. (2021) 'The Infuriating Journey From Pet To Threat: How Bias Undermines Black Women At Work', *Forbes.* [Online] 29th June, Available from: https://www.forbes.com/sites/forbeseq/2021/06/29/the-infuriating-journey-from-pet-to-threat-how-bias-undermines-black-women-at-work/ [Accessed 22/10/21].

Epp, A. M., & Dobson, K. S. (2010) The evidence base for cognitive-behavioral therapy. In K. S. Dobson (Ed.), *Handbook of cognitive-behavioral therapies* (pp. 39–73). Guilford Press.

FundingGuru (2018) *National Study: 62% of UK adults experiencing 'imposter syndrome' at work.* [Online]. Available from: https:/www.fundingguru.com/blog/imposter-syndrome-at-work [Accessed 05/10/21].

Ghorbanshirodi, S. (2012) The Relationship between Self-Esteem and Emotional Intelligence with Imposter Syndrome among Medical Students of Guilan and Heratsi Universities, *Journal of Basic and Applied Scientific Research*, 2 (2), pp. 1793-1802.

Hanks, T. (2016) *Tom Hanks Says Self-Doubt Is 'A High-Wire Act That We All Walk'* [Interview], Fresh Air with T Gross, 26 April 2016.

Harlow, E. (2021) Attachment theory: developments, debates and recent applications in social work, social care and education. *Journal of Social Work Practice,* 35 (1), pp. 79-91.

Health.gov (2021) *Why is getting enough sleep important?* [Online]. Available from: https://health.gov/myhealthfinder/topics/everyday-healthy-living/mental-health-and-relationships/get-enough-sleep#panel-2 [Accessed 15/09/21].

Healthline.com (2020) *Positive Self-Talk: How Talking to Yourself Is a Good Thing*. [Online]. Available from: https://www.healthline.com/health/positive-self-talk#_noHeaderPrefixedContent [Accessed 06/10/21].

Leslie, D., n.d. *What's your unique culture add and online course topic?* [Online]. Available from: https://mycultureadd.com/ [Accessed 11/08/21].

Lukanovich, K. (2020) *Your Body Budget: 3 Key Self-Care Elements for Strong Healthy Clients!* [Online]. Available from: https://www.thecoachingtoolscompany.com/balanced-body-budget-3-essential-elements-of-self-care-karen-lukanovich/ [Accessed 19/06/21].

Lufkin, B. (2021) 'The 'coronasomnia' phenomenon keeping you from getting sleep' *BBC,* [Online] 25th January. Available from: https://www.bbc.com/worklife/article/20210121-the-coronasomnia-phenomenon-keeping-us-from-getting-sleep [Accessed 15/09/21].

McClain, S., Beasley, S. T., Jones, B., Awosogba, O., Jackson, S., and Cokley, K. (2016) An Examination of the Impact of Racial and Ethnic Identity, Impostor Feelings, and Minority Status Stress on the Mental Health of Black College Students, *Journal of Multicultural Counseling and Development,* 44, pp. 101-117.

McGee, E. (2021 'Impostor Syndrome? No. Just racism.', *University World News.* [Online] 5th June. Available from: https://www.universityworldnews.com/post.php?story=20210531104710417 [Accessed 19/11/21].

McKinsey & Company (2021) *Women in the Workplace* [PDF], Retrieved: 2 October, 2015, from: https://wiw-report.s3.amazonaws.com/Women_in_the_Workplace_2021.pdf

Nance-Nash, S. (2020) Why imposter syndrome hits women and women of colour harder. *BBC.* [Online] 28th July. Available from: https://www.bbc.com/worklife/article/20200724-why-imposter-syndrome-hits-women-and-women-of-colour-harder [Accessed 15/09/21].

Open University (2019) *The Zone of proximal development (ZPD).* [Online]. Available from: https://www.open.edu/openlearn/languages/understanding-language-and-learning/content-section-6 [Accessed 13/10/21].

Peteet, B. J., Montgomery, L., and Weekes, J. C. (2015) Predictors of Imposter Phenomenon among Talented Ethnic Minority Undergraduate Students, *The Journal of Negro Education*, 84 (2), pp. 175-186.

Positive Psychology (2021) *What is Positive Self-Talk? (Incl. Examples).* [Online]. Available from: https://positivepsychology.com/positive-self-talk/ [Accessed 15/09/21].

Prasad, P. (2019) The Difference Between Sexism and Misogyny, and Why It Matters. *The Swaddle.* [Online] 1st October. Available from: https://theswaddle.com/difference-between-sexism-and-misogyny/ [Accessed 06/10/21].

RobertsonCooper (2021) *A guide to resilience and resilience training.* [Online]. Available from: https://www.robertsoncooper.com/blog/resilience-and-resilience-training-a-guide/ [Accessed 12/08/21].

Rose, S. n.d. *Do Positive Affirmations Work? A Look at the Science.* [Online]. Available from: https://steverosephd.com/do-positive-affirmations-work/ [Accessed 06/10/21].

Sakulku, J., and Alexander, J. (2011) The Impostor Phenomenon, *International Journal of Behavioural Science*, 6 (1), pp. 75-97.

September, A. N., McCarrey, M., Baranowsky A., Parent C., and Schindler. D. (2001) The Relation between Well-being, Impostor Feelings, and Gender Role Orientation among University Students. *The Journal of Social Psychology,* 14, pp. 218- 232.

Sharma, N., Chakrabarti, S., and Grover, S. (2016) Gender differences in caregiving among family - caregivers of people with mental illnesses, *World Journal of Psychiatry,* 6 (1), pp. 7-17.

Simon, S. (2017) '25 Stars Who Suffer from Imposter Syndrome', *InStyle.* [Online]. 8th December. Available from: https://www.instyle.com/celebrity/stars-imposter-syndrome? [Accessed 06/10/21].

Single Parents on Holiday (2020) *Single Parent Statistics: UK Facts and Figures 2019.* [Online]. Available from: https://www.singleparentsonholiday.co.uk/single-parent-statistics-new-facts-and-figures/ [Accessed 22/10/21].

Stallings, E. (2020) When Black women Go From Office Pet to Office Threat. *Zora Medium.* [Online]. 16th January. Available from: https://zora.medium.com/when-black-women-go-from-office-pet-to-office-threat-83bde710332e [Accessed 22/10/21].

Statista (2016) *Who's Getting The Most Sleep?* [Online]. Available from: https://www.statista.com/chart/4845/countries-in-which-people-are-getting-the-most-sleep/ [Accessed 19/06/21].

Study.com (2020) *Pluralistic Ignorance.* [Online]. Available from: https://study.com/academy/lesson/pluralistic-ignorance-definition-examples-quiz.html [Accessed 25/05/20].

Swinkels, J., van Tilburg, T., Verbakel,E., and van Groenou, M. B. (2019) Explaining the Gender Gap in the Caregiving Burden of Partner Caregivers, *Journals of Gerontology: Social Sciences,* 74 (2), pp. 309-317.

Thomas, K. M. (2013) *Women of Color in the STEM Disciplines* [PowerPoint slides], from Gender Summit 2013. Available from: https://gender-summit.com/images/GS3NA_ppts/Thomas.pdf [Accessed 22/10/201].

Trudy (2014) *Explanation of Misogynoir.* [Online]. Available from: https://www.gradientlair.com/post/84107309247/define-misogynoir-anti-black-misogyny-moya-bailey-coined [Accessed 10/11/21].

Tulshyan, R, and Burey, J. (2021) Stop Telling Women They Have Imposter Syndrome. *Harvard Business Review.* [Online] 11th February. Available from: https://hbr.org/2021/02/stop-telling-women-they-have-imposter-syndrome [Accessed 19/11/21].

UN Womens (2021) *How Covid-19 Impacts Women And Girls.* [Online]. Available from: https://interactive.unwomen.org/multimedia/explainer/covid19/en/index.html?gclid=Cj0KCQjw6NmHBhD2ARIsAI3hrM3OGVNSMrReUWyRyUNAmpJVLolHP9NeGrJMzJE8o5rvqqKs609NoqUaAqagEALw_wcB [Accessed 06/10/21].

VandenBos, G. R. (2015) *American Psychological Association (APA) Dictionary of Psychology.* 2nd ed. Washington DC: American Psychological Association.

Wiest, B. (2018) How To Get Into The "Zone Of Genius" And Unlock Your Highest Potential. *Forbes.* [Online] 26th September. Available from: https://www.forbes.com/sites/briannawiest/2018/09/26/how-to-get-into-the-zone-of-genius-and-unlock-your-highest-potential/ [Accessed 25/10/21].

Wood, J. V., Perunovic, W. Q. E., and Lee, J. W. (2009) Positive Self-Statements: Power for Some, Peril for Others, *Psychological Science,* 20 (7), pp. 860-866.

Young, V. (2011) *The Secret Thoughts of Successful Women: Why Capable People Suffer From the Impostor Syndrome and How to Thrive in Spite of It.* Crown Business: New York.

Zhou, M., & Lin, W. (2016) Adaptability and Life Satisfaction: The Moderating Role of Social Support. *Frontiers in Psychology*, 7, pp. 1-7.

About the Author

Vanetta Morrison is an Emotional Wealth Strategist and Director of 'The Blueprint Way' - an online coaching and counselling service whose mission is to help Black & Brown women develop and maintain their emotional wealth, so they can thrive, from the inside out.

An ACC (Association of Christian Counsellors) accredited counsellor, Vanetta has worked with diverse clients, focusing on anxiety & depression, abuse & trauma, impostor syndrome and grief & loss.

As a mental health consultant, Vanetta also runs corporate and private workshops on Mastering Impostor Syndrome.

Vanetta is also an experienced life & career coach, leveraging 12+ years of leadership, management and psychology experience and facilitating significant individual and organisational successes; both in the Higher Education and charity sector.

To connect with Vanetta and find out more about her services, visit her website: **https://blueprintway.com/services/**

CPSIA information can be obtained
at www.ICGtesting.com
Printed in the USA
BVHW042259031022
648612BV00002B/16

9 781739 69300